T0266744

DARREN O'DONNELL

SOCIAL ACUPUNCTURE

A GUIDE TO SUICIDE, PERFORMANCE AND UTOPIA

COACH HOUSE BOOKS
TORONTO

copyright © Darren O'Donnell, 2006

first edition, third printing, January 2008

Please feel free to contact the author at darren@mammalian.ca.

Published with the assistance of the Canada Council for the Arts and the Ontario Arts Council. Coach House Books also appreciates the support of the Government of Ontario through the Ontario Book Publishing Tax Credit program and the Government of Canada through the Book Publishing Industry Development Program.

LIBRARY AND ARCHIVES CANADA CATALOGUING IN PUBLICATION

O'Donnell, Darren, 1965-
Social acupuncture : a guide to suicide, performance and utopia /
Darren O'Donnell.

Includes the author's play, A suicide-site guide to the city.
Includes bibliographical references.
ISBN-13: 978-1-55245-170-0
ISBN-10: 1-55245-170-4
I. O'Donnell, Darren, 1965- A suicide-site guide to the city. II.
Title.

PS8579.D64S63 2006   C818'.6   C2006-902084-1

to Yvonne

TABLE OF CONTENTS

SOCIAL ACUPUNCTURE

PART ONE
LIFE IN THE SHIT FACTORY

FLUORESCENT LIGHT, WALKING IN CIRCLES AND TALKING TO CAB DRIVERS

The world is a collapsing shit factory. War is total and people are being murdered and tortured in our name every day. Real political engagement is boring and labour intensive, and it involves too much fluorescent light. Activism is hard work, but, honestly, its impenetrably Byzantine internecine weirdness is particularly preposterous in a sector that's trying to build a movement.

I would laugh if I weren't so busy contemplating suicide. I enjoy my privilege; I think everyone should have some. I even enjoy a good demonstration now and again, but not because I have much hope that any good will come of it – if the millions gathered on February 15, 2003, to protest the impending invasion of Iraq can't make a difference, what can? I enjoy demos because they're nice social opportunities. I prefer chatting to chanting, and I hate being cold. I'm a wimp. And I don't like walking in circles. On the other hand, I like fighting with cops, occupying abandoned buildings and throwing cobblestones at Queen's Park. But we're at the wrong moment in history for all that; too many of us are too busy fighting each other and nothing much is going to happen until we get that sorted out. Besides, while the symbolism of a night in jail does offer a bit of a thrill, it doesn't represent anything resembling resistance.

So what's an angry, stupid, white idiot pervert asshole jerkoff supposed to do? I keep trying this voting thing but that seems to be going nowhere. I could write some articles, but I can't shake the feeling that everybody already knows, that critical mass has been achieved – we're all just hung up, distracted by petty details, while all around the shit is hitting the fan. I can squabble about the minutiae of peak-oil theory or pronounce righteously that Empire is here, there, everywhere;

I can hope for some kind of spiralling escalation of insurrections that will spill out of the Parisian suburbs or explode in response to the indignation and horror of New Orleans. I can agree that police forces on every continent are preparing for urban warfare against their own populations. I can talk about all the weird tales circulating about 9/11 or watch with a sick certainty what's unfolding with respect to Iran; I can agree that white supremacy still explains so much of it all. I can leave town and try to find a place where more progressive things are happening, but they're not my struggles, I don't speak the language and, besides, I'm lazy. I know I'm complicit; I try to recycle, shop correctly, hire equitably and strike up friendly conversations with cab drivers, but it all seems like a stupid, offensive joke I'm either perpetrating or the butt of, and I'm too confused or too stupid to tell the difference. I'm well-read, I have my finger on the pulse of this and that; I know big words and I sort of know how to use them, if not how to spell them. I want to be engaged in world events. But, essentially, I'm a twerp, a powerless pipsqueak, strong enough to push around a few of my dazed and less-informed comrades, and while that does provide a bit of a thrill, it's hardly a long-term strategy. Shit, it's not even a short-term strategy; it's just enough of a narcissism of small differences to prevent me from capitulating to my real desire to kick back, put up my feet and go for dinner at McDonald's – say whatever you like, the fries are *good*.

CREATIVITY, ALZHEIMER'S AND MY NEXT P-R-O-J-E-C-T

There's been a lot of buzz about creativity and how it's going to make everything okay, so why does all this chit-chat makes me so fucking nervous? When unabashed and unfettered creativity seemed like an idea emanating from our end of things, something we did in the interstices of the city, I had this crazy belief that, like weeds cracking through the concrete, these efforts would begin to erode those circuits of capital that were keeping us subjugated, isolated, atomized, bored and sad. But just like Big Bucks figured out how to recoup the liberatory individualism of the sixties, all of this culture-jamming seems to have been scooped and recouped, brought back into the profit-driven fold, like an Alzheimer's patient gently guided by the elbow back into the safety of the locked ward. Now we surf from cultural event to cultural event, this modest purring economic engine providing plenty of beer sales, the line of cabs outside our favourite boutique hotel testimony to the power of culture to grease the wheels of commerce.

I feel tricked. Of course, it's easy for stupid people to feel tricked – that's how we avoid feeling stupid. How did I end up spending so much time believing that culture had some revolutionary potential? What was I thinking?

Was that me who dressed like a businessman and went down to the financial district to dance in the streets, convinced that it had the power to affect the withered souls there? Was I so arrogant? Did I join a Situationist International reading group and walk aimlessly through the city scanning my body for how capitalist planning guides my desires? Did I hang fake money on trees on Bay Street to make some point about something or other, organize 7 a.m. parties on the subway to jar the squares out of their stupor and provide them with a glimpse of a truly liberated soul? Did I really believe the People would prefer my self-conscious manic glee to the quiet, meditative clickity-clack of the subway? Did I spray random chunks of concrete with colour, claiming to heal the soul of the beleaguered city? Did I really construct plastic structures atop exhaust grates to critique the homelessness generated by neoliberal reforms? Did I really organize talking parties for strangers and play Spin the Bottle with a room full of adults?

Did I call it activism? That was me, I swear, or someone who looked an awful lot like me. What was I thinking? How did my head get so fat?

My next project is seven forty-five-foot-high white letters spelling the word P-R-O-J-E-C-T that I'm going to weigh with gold and sink to the bottom of Lake Ontario. For the project after that, I'm going to swallow a string of golden anal beads embossed with the letters P-R-O-J-E-C-T and then ride the Zipper until I puke them up. After that I'll hire seven children, adorn each with a gold pendant of a single letter – P-R-O-J-E-C-T – and get them to walk with me everywhere as they chant the word over and over. And then I'm getting colon cancer and dying. At least, that's what I've said on my grant applications. But you know the creative process: a streetcar could hit me even as I write this.

THEATRE, EMBARRASSMENT AND COMMODIFICATION

I do most of my work in theatre not for any good reason but because of a few bad choices, some success, an obsessive need for attention and because I hadn't noticed that the possibility of an activist theatre capable of direct civic engagement has more or less evaporated.

After I graduated from theatre school and moved to Toronto, it quickly became obvious that acting wasn't the locus of creativity I had been led to believe. Interesting work in theatre was rare, in television it was non-existent and most film work involved small, dull roles in American movies of the week. I played a paramedic, an alien, a bystander and someone who loves pasta but doesn't have the time to make it himself. I had spent most of my time in theatre school hiding in the library and reading Grotowski's *Towards a Poor Theatre*, so when I was introduced to Buddies in Bad Times' Rhubarb! Festival, I recognized it as a place where I might find like-minded people to push some personal and creative boundaries. It was exciting. Sky Gilbert and Tim Jones had managed to nurture a vibrant, socially engaged community of perverts and weirdos who were creating good work. I formed my first company, Pow Pow Unbound, with Wendy Agnew, Sigrid Johnson and Stephen Seabrook. We did a few interesting shows, including *A Horrible Night of a Man of War*, *Field* and *Stage/Groove*, and then went our separate ways. I formed my current company, Mammalian Diving Reflex, in 1993 and have been writing and producing work since then.

I'm embarrassed that I've stuck with it for so long and will probably continue until I can find something else to do. It feels a little too late for a career in a more socially relevant field – besides, like I said, I'm kind of dumb, I love attention and I would survive in an ordinary workplace about as long as it takes to say 'my anus is the new black' before getting knocked out by some harassment or incompetence charge. And I would deserve it: I'm an idiot. I guess I could change, though I've only ever managed small, temporary changes. I once stopped eating for a few weeks to drop some pounds before a performance but quickly returned to old habits, eating a doughnut during the curtain call. I'm addicted to all my bad habits, including theatre, even as they remain only remotely connected to sensations that I vaguely remember providing me with pleasure.

While all art is suspect, theatre is looking particularly sketchy. With the proliferation of biennials, music and film festivals and design events, at least you can accuse other forms of selling out; all you can accuse theatre of doing is nothing. Examining the fading of theatre as a form that once held the promise of a democratic forum, like the examination of any organ that's falling apart, can yield valuable insights about the wider – in this case socio-cultural – system. I never understood how the practitioners of traditional Chinese medicine managed to acquire such subtle, nuanced and subjective understandings of the body until my own started to fall apart. *Ohhhh*, so *that's* Damp Heat in the Lower Burner. Watching theatre – a form that has always had an intimate association with public discourse and democracy – struggle to maintain cultural relevance can help us understand the dysfunction of the wider social body. The particular aspects of theatre that have prevented it from making a graceful transition into the twenty-first century are challenged in much of the public arena.

Over the course of the twentieth century, theatre has been eclipsed by the other time-based representational forms: film, television and now gaming and other online activities. Theatre practitioners tried to hold on, often resorting to snobbery and a wistful attachment to the classical canon. But in terms of contemporary cultural relevance, the European tradition of representational theatre as an active part of a civic discourse is more or less finished. That's not to say that hanging out together and experiencing constructed time-based events is history, but it does mean that a definitive break with certain traditions needs to occur if we want to salvage the aspects of theatre that contribute to a healthy and vibrant exchange of ideas.

Theatre suffers from the economic realities of the day, which are unable to sustain a forum where actual bodies encounter one another. Capitalism is not here to stay, but until it goes, theatre will be sidelined simply because it can't be commodified, capitalism's most basic requirement. It's impossible to duplicate and mass-produce theatre. Recording the event is next to impossible, and the published playscripts, while a commodity within the industry, hold little interest outside the field. You can point to some products like the big international musicals, but these exist in a different economy of scale and in no way shed any light on the opportunities for mid-range producers. Theatre production, at that magnitude, has little to do with the work itself; it's part of a larger package that offers tourists a big-city/Broadway/West End experience. Mid-sized companies cannot duplicate this without the heavy capital necessary to generate a huge buzz.

Theatre's most disabling trait, from the point of view of commodification, is that it requires the very expensive prospect of the creators and the consumers being in the same room at the same time – and not just any room, but a theatre. This makes it unique among the arts; I can think of no other form with these kinds of restrictions. Even performance art and dance can be documented without sacrificing too much of the original impulse.

The uncommodifiability of theatre means it has remained largely a local phenomenon, with theatre artists isolated from artists working in other places and other media. A recent art school graduate can make a modest film or video and have it shown around the world. In theatre, the young artist has to invest years before touring becomes an option, except at the level of the Fringe circuit, where work is often lost in the melee and financial risk looms large. Even then, the economics of touring preclude all but the very successful from accessing more than a few locales. Theatre is caught in an eddy, in a redundant conversation with itself, out of the loop of the cultural, philosophical, political and aesthetic developments in other forms. Information-age capitalism, with its demand that cultural products be digitized and circulated via electronic networks, has left theatre gasping for intelligence, relevance and currency.

SNOBBERY REPRESENTATION
AND DAMP HEAT IN THE LOWER BURNER

But while technological advancements and the currents of history are largely to blame, we can't overlook the individual responsibility of the theatre artist, who should be chastized for her reluctance to admit the reality of changing economics and aesthetics. There's been snobbery among theatre practitioners, some bizarre headspace that keeps us focused on the classical canon, with Shakespeare as the gold standard. Imagine if things were similar in the visual arts: artists continually representing their classical canon, these interpretations often relying on contemporary costuming to help audiences make thematic connections between then and now. Imagine seeing the *Mona Lisa* over and over – this time dressed as a flapper, next time as a Nazi, then as a hippie, then as an emo girl. It's an absurd idea, yet Romeo and Juliet keep on killing themselves again and again and again, sometimes dressed like b-boys. Actors covet these roles; they long to speak those lines, believing, for some reason, that mastering the classics signifies some artistic pinnacle. Innovative young practitioners capable of moving the form in new directions simply don't have the resources to dislodge this obsession with the classics. Unlike popular music, which cut itself loose from parental apron strings decades ago, there is very little in the way of popular or alternative theatre that is not imaginatively and fiscally beholden to the past. Mostly this is a problem of economics – it doesn't cost much to buy a guitar, practice in your parents' basement and do a show at Sneaky Dee's. But theatre costs real money: rehearsal and performance space is expensive, and nobody spends money getting shit-faced on beer while we're performing. So, like any capital-intensive project, theatre has had to remain within a system of companies with buildings, which are inevitably institutions just on the brink of survival, too frightened to invest in any real risk, hoping always to capitalize on past successes. And who is more successful than Shakespeare? The Fringe Festival offered an antidote to all this, with lots of innovative work appearing in the early years. But with no real way to be economically viable, the Fringe – both in Edinburgh and

North America – rapidly devolved into little more than a trade show, with teams of artists constantly losing money in the hopes that their show would become the next *Da Kink in My Hair* or *The Drowsy Chaperone* – these exceptions doing little more than proving the rule.

The classical canon and traditional approaches to representation still hold the theatrical imagination captive. Most theatre still hasn't managed to dispense with coherent, pithy and supposedly interesting characters whose lives occur incident by incident. Presenting false possibilities of self-knowing – even among nominally postmodern dramatists – still dominates: characters' lives are summed up, they understand their various shortcomings and blind spots, and they're offered some sort of redemption, whether or not they choose to take it. And if they don't, then, at the very least, the audience is offered that possibility. Representational work – work that derives its meaning from the portrayal of other people in other places doing other things – still dominates, imposing its inherent limitations around the construction of transparent subjectivities and the illusory possibility of an objective position from which observation can occur. It also brings along its tyrannical emphasis on narrative; it's a dramaturgical cliché that the fundamental component of theatre is story and storytelling. While stories may be one way to get the job done, they're not the only way; stories are simply one tool among many. What theatre is *really* about – like any other form – is generating affect, and that's it. Feelings. And, if things go well, quickly following feelings will be thoughts. Stories certainly can do this, but they're not the only thing to do it, and they're no longer always the best way to do it. Yet representational narrative continues to dominate, keeping the experience sheltered from the possibility of a direct encounter between audience and artist, between bodies in the same room at the same time. But this is a Damp Heat in the Lower Burner moment;

by understanding what's gone wrong, we might find an answer. Perhaps we can turn theatre's liability – the proximity of creator and consumer – into an asset.

REALITY, SPONTANEITY AND ANIMALS ONSTAGE

The reality movement in television and the explosion of interest in documentary film have shifted the terrain, with representational drama ceding a significant portion of its audience. Part of this shift is economic – it's cheaper to make reality-based work – but it also stems from the genuine interest we have in the real tribulations of real people. Postmodern consciousness recognizes the performativity of real life and the sociological currents evident in almost every gesture; the ubiquitous corporeal dynamics of race/class/gender/etc. This has yielded an appreciation of the real as a potentially more sophisticated, revealing and rewarding realm than that of carefully constructed, contrived and wrought fictional representations. Theatre has always known a live animal onstage will inevitably be more interesting than even the most brilliant performance, even as it has ignored the ramifications of this insight. So, while film and television capitalize on this interest in the real, it's theatre, paradoxically, that can generate the real *for real*. Real reality is much more likely to be found in the theatre, where the audience is within coughing distance. Yet most theatre is still ensconced behind the fourth wall: those few postmodern works that do take into account the presence of the audience still keep things under strict control with carefully memorized text, tight light cues and no meaningful audience interface. But the innocent gestures of the spontaneous will always tell us complex and politically charged things about this very moment, giving theatre artists the opportunity to find rigorous ways to generate and frame it. That's the challenge, with theatre's addiction to a very particular understanding of a rigidly rehearsed virtuosity standing in its way. It's easy with film and TV – you just edit out the dull shit, focusing on the telling spontaneous moments. This is not so easy when the interactions are live, and particularly so if they involve audience interaction. There will always be annoying fumbles and distractions, and a final product that doesn't have the same concision that editing allows.

The path to a rigorous participatory theatre is fraught with dorkiness, earnestness, amateurism, social work and therapy. It's a minefield. And no one can be blamed for feeling squeamish or repulsed by the notion. We like our work rehearsed and we like it well rehearsed, like a nice charbroiled steak from Denny's. The question for the theatre artist anxious to break with debilitating habits of the past is how to create thoughtful, rigorous work while allowing for the unknown, the unexpected and the awkward – how to find meaning in qualities other than virtuosity and razzle-dazzle. In a beautiful and revolutionary irony, the real magic of theatre may ultimately be in its banality.

REAL REALITY, DEMOCRACY AND DISCOMFORT

The struggle of theatre for social relevance without the benefit of easy commodification is instructive for all forms; it points to avenues for establishing, sustaining and maintaining the relevance of art in general. If participation is the key for theatre, it can be applied with success to many other forms. Our burgeoning penchant for interactivity and forums for healthy discussion is sustained or fortified largely by the hype around the Internet and other participatory interfaces. Though there will always be the suspicion that it's still about sales, the media is certainly democratizing: the forums solic-iting comment are many, and the discussions that follow a given article on, say, the *Globe and Mail*'s website are often of more interest than the article itself. The article may be the catalyst, but more and more, the discussion that follows – as loose, stupid and obnoxious as it can sometimes be – provides a much better sense of where things are at. The deluge of racist diatribes that followed the recent coverage of the Supreme Court's ruling allowing Sikh students to carry kirpans was a creepy reminder that stupid, salivating bigotry lies mere microns – if that – beneath the artifice of Canadian tolerance. A revealing interactiveness, even if it reveals ugliness – maybe *especially* if it reveals ugliness – is the order of the day, and that's a good thing.

So if theatre's relevance as a democratic forum lies in its potential as a participatory form, then how will this look? How can it play out? The answers are legion and can be glimpsed in the visual-art world, with its turn toward the social and its plethora of projects that bring people together and induce interactivity. But before we get too excited, we have to return to the question of my P-R-O-J-E-C-T projects and the role of art and art-making. If our work – interactive or not – is to have any real effect, we must resist being pulled into the gravity of a horny capital's need for content for its information networks and the city's need for superficial cultural activity that does nothing to question socio-economic dynamics. It's been fun to experience the last few years as art production has begun to incorporate increasingly sophisticated approaches to fostering dialogue and we've seen the proliferation of events designed to create networks, friendships and communities. But this, too, now seems about to unravel with its co-optation by a manic and hollow civic boosterism. The hype that surrounds Richard Florida's book *The Rise of the Creative Class* and his assertion that urban economic development is dependent on the activity of creative types can be seen in initiatives like Toronto's Live with Culture campaign. This nominal support for culture and the plethora of activities it encourages, while perhaps fun for the kids on a lazy Sunday, does nothing to attend to any of the real indicators of civic health: housing, public transit, employment, immigrant services, etc. As artists being recruited to contribute to this Creative City concept, we must be careful not to simply create projects that glorify the sweet, whimsical and easy – projects that reinforce enclaves of race, culture, age and gender. We need to start engaging with unease and discomfort. Art shows and articles abound that invite critical and utopian considerations of the possibilities of the city's future, but rarely do the suggestions or the work take themselves seriously or rigorously engage with policy.

I was being rude in my earlier litany of suspect projects, referencing friends and associates like Free Dance Lessons, the Toronto Public Space Committee's *Better Way* exhibit, the Urban Beautification Brigade, the City Beautification Ensemble, the October Group and my own project, *The Talking Creature*. It's clear from this list that the impulse to engage with the social is strong: artists are keen to generate works that activate the public sphere by either questioning old ways of being or proposing new ones. My concern is that the primary purpose of these projects is to provide a release valve for the pent-up frustration the artist is feeling toward social realities; I worry that we prefer fun and whimsy to rigorous social engagement. All of those projects are good and important – but only as a start. The stakes must be raised, an engagement fostered that takes the work far from these comfortable circuits of galleries, clubs and events, far from the familiar dichotomous thinking in simplistic and dualistic challenges to the squares on Bay Street or to Office Drone culture.

As we were doing our culture-jamming, engaging with the rhetoric of social activism, righteously demonstrating that another world is possible, we inadvertently began to develop an Art Drone culture, a new kind of rat race, fuelled by the promise of better days, party times and the delusion that the creative networks we were fostering were something more than simply fun. We recoiled from the ennui of political irrelevance, wanting to believe we could engage meaningfully, but rarely did we have the courage to accept that discomfort, confusion and powerlessness is our reality. We preferred, instead, to pretend. Fun is fun, after all, and you can't blame us for trying. But there is the need for an understanding of art that goes not only beyond pleasant aesthetics, but beyond even typical ideas of creativity and imagination, directly engaging with the civic sphere. An aesthetic that can work directly with the institutions of civil society – an aesthetic of civic engagement. An aesthetic that says: Okay, so you want to make culture and creativity a central part of civic life? Fine. Then I want in on the institutions that form – at ground level – the fabric of the city. I want to use these as material in my art practice.

'It would be wrong, in a society in which every discussion of basic principles has been lost, to expect that something like art can make decisive changes. Folksongs don't rescue whales; "Stop AIDS" posters don't stop the spread of the disease; and Klaus Staeck's agitprop posters have hardly hindered speculation in the housing market. Did Picasso's *Guernica* do anything for the tormented residents of that city? It remains a monument, a ritual of grief and an admission that the power to effect anything with art is limited.' – WochenKlausur[1]

The realization that art can do very little to make the world a better place is a lot like the realization that the individual is relatively powerless. It may even be the same realization.

The political left – especially those of us working in the cultural sectors – claims communitarian objectives, but it has, paradoxically, invested a lot in the idea that the individual is powerful and that one's individual actions make a difference in the world. But while this may be true in a very limited way, it's mostly false.

Artists and other cultural workers on the left need to believe this to keep nihilism at bay during this time of retreat and reorganization. But exerting what little power we have as individuals to live responsibly in an irresponsible world has negligible results, often serving merely to placate a guilty conscience. And even this guilt is just another by-product of the market, fuelling compulsions as ill-considered as that of keeping ahead of the pack on the latest whatever. Efforts to address world inequities through art, while well-intentioned, are devastatingly naïve. Art has lost this round. Decisively.

In *A Brief History of Neoliberalism*, David Harvey characterizes the last thirty years of globalization as a radical reshaping of world economic relations that aims to reinstate a global upper class – a class that saw its share of the pie scaled down by post–World War II Keynesian economics.[2] This reshaping, initiated in the seventies, has included the dismantling of the welfare state, decisive hits to labour and the creation of what post-Marxist Antonio Negri calls the warfare state,[3] and it has insistently pestered art. On one hand, it has scaled back state funding, and on the other, invited art to step up to the challenge of commodification. Art-making is now an entrepreneurial endeavour, and many artists are eagerly entering the market, with, for example, retail outlets dedicated exclusively to multiples and the Internet as a portal for the distribution of artistic merchandise. And while the idea of an artist as a businessperson melding personal vision with market trends may annoy some, it's perhaps less bothersome than the vision of the artist as an individual who, somehow separate from the dirty world, listens to the true music of his or her heart and offers it up untainted and uncompromised.

Absurdly enough, capital accomplished this easy reshaping by recouping the revolutionary ideals of the sixties. The notion of freedom has been turned back against itself, fostering creative and flexible workplaces and work situations. At first, the freelance economy, working from home and telecommuting, seemed like a reasonable antidote to the nine-to-five grind. But freelancers, particularly those of us working in the cultural sectors, where much of the product we generate happens in the imagination and the evenings, quickly find ourselves working nine-to-nine and beyond, checking email first thing in the morning and last thing at night.

This emphasis on individual freedoms also makes islands of us. It's great to be an autonomous individual, but it's a short leap to a situation in which that same individual is cut off from more collective, social endeavours. Even that socializing that does occur happens under the banner of consumption. Nicolas Bourriaud, in *Relational Aesthetics*, laments the current condition of communication, claiming, 'before long, it will not be possible to maintain relationships between people outside [these] trading areas. So here we are summonsed to talk about things around a duly priced drink, as a symbolic form of contemporary human relations.' And it's true. For many of us it's difficult to spend time with a friend without the threat of consumption: let's go for a beer, a coffee, for dinner, a movie. 'The relationship between people,' writes

Bourriaud, 'as symbolized by goods or replaced by them, and signposted by logos, has to take on extreme and clandestine forms, if it is to dodge the empire of predictability.'[4]

THE RELATIONAL, REVOLUTION AND FUN

One response to this incessant commodification is the explosion of artistic practices that induce encounters between people, replacing an object-based art practice with one dedicated to generating relationships.

In my city, Toronto, there has been a proliferation of this kind of work, which has been variously termed 'relational,' 'littoral' and 'dialogical.' Free Dance Lessons, a project by Paige Graitland and Day Millman offers dance lessons to an unsuspecting public in atypical locations: on the street, in front of a grocery store and in the subway. Shawn Micallef, Gabe Sawhney and James Roussel's [murmur] project invites people to record verbal stories about specific locations in the city that can be heard on the web, by cellphone anytime, an ear-shaped sign providing the access code. Simone Moir's *Video Store Make-Out* invited the viewer/participant to a series of make-out sessions at video stores on Valentine's Day 2004, without providing any means to determine who was there to make out and who was there shopping for videos; it became an exercise in navigating desire in a relatively public space.

In all this activity, Bourriaud still sees the modernist impulse to refashion the world into a better place; unlike the twentieth-century avant-garde, however, today's artists have abandoned idealistic, revolutionary and teleological aspirations and, instead, investigate the simple interactions between people.[5] This is a good thing when you consider the myriad uses to which market capitalism has put those revolutionary impulses. Revolution has been so thoroughly – if perhaps temporarily and wishfully – appropriated by Big Money, that it's a tough term to use with a straight face.

It's not that the need for revolution has abated, however. Dissatisfaction with the current global shit factory hasn't gone anywhere – the litany of horrors is getting deeper and the avenues for meaningful engagement fewer and fewer. The activist left isn't offering much help with this problem, suffering as it does from a self-hating narcissism of small differences that sees it erecting its own barriers to wider participation, the empire of cool haunting it as it haunts any group. It's the same tired old story of divided and conquered. Most artists, finding little time or incentive to get their analysis up to an acceptable speed, will always fall short, their presence often an awkward addition to any coalition. So, instead, artists have backed away from direct political action, the desire to change the world morphing into efforts to 'learn to inhabit the world in a better way, instead of trying to construct it based on preconceived ideas of historical evolution.'[6] One of Bourriaud's favourite examples is Ontario College of Art and Design-educated Rirkrit Tiravanija, whose piece *Untitled (Tomorrow Is Another Day)* illustrates that 'the role of artworks is no longer to form imaginary and utopian realities, but to actually be ways of living and models of action within the existing real.'[7] Tiravanija situated a replica of his New York apartment in European galleries and offered 24/7 access; the public was invited to hang out with Rirkrit, chat, make and eat food and use the toilet. Bourriaud feels this kind of work creates microtopias, small enclaves carrying the possibility of freedom. And there's no doubt that these kinds of events are FUN, just like a utopia is supposed to be. It's fun to chill, have a little snack, jiggle the toilet handle and change the world at the very same time.

But some people are not convinced. The eggheads at the European Institute for Progressive Cultural Policies take issue, feeling that turning microtopias into art by making them visible renders the microtopias ineffective. Their November 2005 symposium in Barcelona featured Claire Bishop, one of the more consistent critics of Bourriaud and his crew, who feels that efforts to create conviviality and supposedly democratic spaces tend to reinforce already existing social circuits – complete with the same exclusivities, cliques and in-crowds. According to Bishop, Bourriaud ignores the fact that a vibrant social sphere is one that can openly acknowledge and even generate antagonisms – that democracy is dependent on friction rather than feel-good.[8]

I'm reminded of the sentiment of First Nations activist Ward Churchill when he speaks of the tendency of activists – which we can stretch to include artists who are trying to deal honestly with (if not change) the world – to want to remain within their comfort zones: 'There's a whole feel-good ethic out there. It's not [to] effect any substantive change. It's to bear moral witness to make the person feel good, to assuage their conscience.'[9]

Churchill explains that there will be no significant change in current economic arrangements without enduring personal discomfort. Bishop, too, thinks little utopias are kidding themselves. Social discomfort, while a pain in the ass to endure, is often necessary if we have any interest in increasing our social intelligence. It's like mental confusion: any learning process must encounter a period of confusion – without it there's no learning. With social intelligence, discomfort and antagonism are hallmarks of a successful encounter.

As an example, Bishop cites Santiago Sierra, whose controversial work with illegal workers and refugees points up and exacerbates social exclusion, forcing the public to acknowledge their complicit relationship with oppressive powers.[10] For *Workers Who Cannot Be Paid, Remunerated to Remain Inside Cardboard Boxes*, Sierra hired Chechnyan asylum seekers to spend the day at a gallery hidden in small cardboard boxes. 'The work does not offer an experience of transcendent human empathy that smooths over the awkward situation before us,' writes Bishop, 'but a pointed racial and economic nonidentification: "this is not me." The persistence of this friction, its awkwardness and discomfort, alerts us to the relational antagonism of Sierra's work.'[11] Bishop contrasts the sweetness of Bourriaud's vision with Sierra's more brutal practice, which refuses to create common communities but instead highlights difference in ways that force undeniable encounters.

I sympathize with Bishop's desire for difficult encounters, but for Sierra's piece to have any resonance at all, there has to be consensus that it's a hot-potato issue: there must be general disagreement about the status of Chechnyan refugees. In many ways, the piece already exists in the real world. The conditions Sierra critiques are visible to all in the first place – otherwise the work has no effect. Its confrontational antagonism only repeats a difficult discussion already happening in other arenas. That it's now happening in a gallery is certainly a good thing, but the questions raised will not likely expand beyond the discussion as it's already occurring with the same content and among the same activists, politicians, journalists, etc. That's not to say the publicity might not do the issue some good; it might get more tongues wagging and expedite a wider social engagement with the issue.

Both Bourriaud's and Bishop's favourite examples represent conversations that are already happening elsewhere now moving into the gallery or under the aegis of art. Bishop says that any old conversation is not enough to introduce democracy; we have to interrogate who is conversing, who isn't and what we are talking about. I agree, but I wonder if there might be another way, a way to induce encounters between individuals where we bring the aegis of art out into the world and use it to blanket traditionally non-artistic activities – activities in which power differentials are at least tacitly acknowledged and the artistic manoeuvre is to either reverse or erase them temporarily in a gesture of antagonism that contributes to rising social intelligence. Could we develop an aesthetic that favours work in which relational situations employ moments of antagonism toward a unification of oppositions in the civic sphere? Could civic engagement – the use of civil institutions as material – create the basis for an artistic practice?

CIVIL SOCIETY, UNFEASIBILITY
AND THE STRATEGIC USE OF THE MYTHOS OF ART

Wikipedia tells us, 'Civil society or civil institutions refers to the totality of voluntary civic and social organizations or institutions which form the basis of a functioning society as opposed to the force-backed structures of a state (regardless of that state's political system).'[12] These institutions of civil society, for some, offer exciting alternatives to or bulwarks against capitalist globalization, avenues for socio-political engagement outside the formal structures of the state. The various institutions of civil society include non-governmental organizations, private voluntary organizations, community-based organizations, civic clubs, trade unions, cultural and religious groups, charities, social and sports clubs, co-operatives, environmental groups, academia, businesses and the media. And if we're willing to expand the notion of art, these institutions and their populations offer the possibility of serving as material in artistic practice.

Gustavo Artigas's *The Rules of the Game*, staged as part of Tijuana/San Diego's inSite 2000, brought two Tijuana high school soccer teams to play against each other while, simultaneously and on the same court, two basketball teams from San Diego competed. Artigas's work becomes a metaphor for the difficult realities of two cultures – American and Mexican – occupying the same space and time. Artigas takes four sports clubs and induces an atypical encounter. The teams do what they ordinarily do, but the context is altered with slight but decisive modifications, so there's an added dimension of challenge, fun and, ultimately, meaning. This lack of significant modification distinguishes an aesthetic of civic engagement from, say, community arts, popular education, intervention or even relational work. Artistic civic engagement, rather than imposing a particular form, tries to remain within the activity flows already occurring in a population or community. In this way, such engagement can be considered even more faithful to the first principle of popular education – to let the learners do the leading.

The Rules of the Game succeeds in drawing attention to the specific situation of the cohabitation of two cultures across a border, but it proves that symbiosis can flow naturally, that the two populations can coexist. *now*'s reviewer writes, 'At first they collide in confusion, but after a few minutes the two games evolve to work with each other, and soon it's a well-choreographed spectacle where goals and baskets are scored in unison.'[13] The piece, even detached from its political context, can still provide politically charged content by proving that differences don't need to be ironed out; two sets of rules, norms and behaviours can exist in the same space at the same time and the difference can serve to unify. In this way, *The Rules of the Game* elucidates what political philosophers Hardt and

Negri describe as 'the Multitude': 'When we approach a different population we are no longer forced to choose between saying either "They are the same as us" or "They are other to us" (as was the case with the discourse on primitives and, to some extent, peasants). The contradictory conceptual couple, identity and difference, is not the adequate framework for understanding the organization of the multitude. ... The anthropology of the multitude is an anthropology of singularity and commonality.'[14]

In Artigas's project, multitude is created, paradoxically, by drawing attention to otherness. This unity of differences is dependent on the intelligence-raising antagonism that Bishop is looking for; in this case, in fact, the differences are also *hair-raising*, as the kids do, initially, collide in confusion. The discomfort of the chaos the young athletes experience, as well as the dissonance experienced by the viewer, is an important but temporary moment in the piece as a whole – a moment that is intended to evaporate before the viewer's eyes.

This kind of work demonstrates and even ritualizes that certain things considered unfeasible can actually happen.

Pushing the envelope of such work is WochenKlausur, an Austrian collective whose interventions exist on the very outer reaches of what is currently considered art, sometimes threatening to tip over into social work. They view art as process-rather than object-based. Over the last thirteen years, their interventions have worked with a variety of institutions, finding creative solutions to a diversity of issues, including the conditions of detainees awaiting deportation, the isolation of mentally disabled older people and reintegration of drug addicts into the workforce.[15] If asked when something should be considered art, they point to the various players responsible for shaping consensus: 'Powerful institutions like museums, schools and media are decisive for what becomes art. ... WochenKlausur's work ... becomes art through its recognition, and that comes about within institutional mechanisms. Every art remains a fully harmless raw material until these mechanisms take this raw material and circulate an opinion about it.'[16]

WochenKlausur's use of art is strategic in a bigger game with higher states. They're attempting to increase the significance of intervening in existing social circumstances, by rehabilitating the very word 'social.' They are looking to reduce the do-gooderism that often surrounds social efforts by re-evaluating them in the context of art. They call upon the mythos of 'art' to help realize something in the political field. This strategy plays particularly on the myth of art as something removed from the dirty dealings of day-to-day, something transcendent. Taking advantage of this erroneous assumption can allow artists access to situations, populations and resources that bar activists with overt agendas, even though the artist may share that agenda. WochenKlausur points out, too, that 'the media reports less about the most exciting social work than about the dullest cultural events,' and so they use media 'in any way [they] can' trying to put pressure on decision-makers.'[17] They're candid about their strategic use of the appellation 'art,' but they maintain that art is what artists say art is. And that's that.

ACTIVISM, THE EMPIRE OF COOL AND THE LIMITS OF CHARITY

Activism as art and activist art are two different things. Activist art is any recognized and accepted form that happens to carry political/polemical content, while activism as art might not look like art and might not involve any pre-existing forms. It is also distinguishable from community arts, where the artist – as emissary of a form such as dancing, singing, painting, video art – shares skills and works with a community to give expression to concerns. All of these approaches have their place and can be effective in their own right, but it's important to be able to distinguish between them.

Rehabilitating the word 'social' by hitching it to art amounts to an attempt to hipify social work. This isn't a bad thing. It's vital to remember the lessons of history, neo-liberalism in particular. Crucial in this respect is a leftist recouping of selfishness. The seventies saw capitalism harness and channel the sixties' demands for individualism, self-expression and autonomy. That we continue to think of the sixties as a golden age of activism is due to the power that was unleashed by this demand for individualism; the power of autonomy has since been harnessed to keep the motors of capital running smoothly. This has been inadvertently encouraged by the anticapitalist artist who tries to resist this by renouncing authorship. The death of the author has led, paradoxically, to what Claire Bishop, in *The Social Turn: Collaboration and its Discontents* calls 'a situation in which not only collectives but also individual artists are praised for their authorial renunciation. And this may explain, to some degree, why socially engaged art has been largely exempt from art criticism.'[18] As activists, it's important that we utilize any and all opportunities to raise awareness of our efforts, taking full responsibility for our work even if that means garnering both praise and criticism. The virtue associated with the disavowal of authorial credit leads down blind alleys where due credit is conflated with the hunger for power.

How can this drive for individualism be resurrected and brought back into the realm of the social, the realm of those of us who yearn for a more equitable distribution of wealth and power? Michael Hardt, in his 2005 Ioan Davies Lecture at York University, *The Politics of Love and Evil in the Multitude*, talked of the need to unify two poles: Charity and Desire.[19]

It's bad manners to engage in an act of charity to increase your own prestige; charity must occur without want, yearning or desire. It's something you do for others, not for yourself – otherwise, it's not charity. This is a popular line of thinking, strongly advocated by, among others, Christ, most famously in the Sermon on the Mount: 'Take heed that ye do not your alms before men, to be seen of them: otherwise ye have no reward of your Father which is in heaven.'[20] While the sermon has some really great advice, this is one spot where it falls flat. We understand the prohibition against being the hypocritical loudmouth who brags about doing good deeds while, in fact, doing nothing. But what about the guy who can walk his talk? Why not let him brag about his good deeds and tell us all what a great time he's having doing them? The rich know all about this, with large-scale acts of philanthropy often bearing the name of the donor. That this triggers the occasional pissing match, like the one between Joey Tanenbaum and Kenneth Thompson over the redesign of the Art Gallery of Ontario, should be considered a good thing. There's nothing wrong with some childish competition if it leads to more resources flowing to endeavours that strengthen the civic sphere.

Bishop doesn't believe in artistic self-sacrifice. 'The discursive criteria of socially engaged art,' she says, 'are at present, drawn from a tacit analogy between anticapitalism and the Christian "good soul." In this schema, self-sacrifice is triumphant: The artist should renounce authorial presence in favor of allowing participants to speak through him or her.'[21] Do-gooderism, as such, merely maintains and reiterates problematic power dynamics by maintaining the offending inequity. A really effective intervention recognizes that improving conditions for others must also somehow improve conditions for yourself. In this way, selfishness is recouped – but in the name of wider social good. All good deeds should also be self-liberating and, as such, worthy of celebration. 'If you're coming to help me, you are wasting your time. But if you have come because your liberation is bound up with mine, then let us work together,'[22] says Lilla Watson, an Australian aboriginal activist and artist. This sentiment rejects acts of charity that do not also improve the well-being of the donor.

So, what benefit can accrue to the artist engaged in social fortification? Working to make the world a better place should be a reward in itself, but these kinds of transformations occur very slowly with tangible results taking place too far in the future to provide most artists the incentive to engage. It's nice to feel a few material results for our labours and – considering the state of the world – we need to utilize any incentives we can find.

In all artistic practice – even that of civic engagement – a by-product is social capital: fame. At bottom, the desire for fame is the desire to be loved unconditionally by a lot of people, most of whom you don't know. It's the desire to be able to be yourself wherever you are and have that expression respected and supported. Fame offers a bit of that. It's social capital – the ability to tap the resources of a wider community simply because you are known. And as such, fame shouldn't be underestimated as a potentially progressive social force and political tool. The concern that fame is powerful only because so few people have it is based on the misconception that that there's only so much of it to go around. And while this may be true in large economies, where recognition is tied to a share of the consumer's dollar, it's not true in smaller but politically significant ponds such as the civic sphere. There's always room for more fame in that realm because the activities are proximate, more collaborative and not tied to massive amounts of capital. In this register, fame is very close to love, because it has to involve and sustain so much one-on-one contact. The idea that fame or love is a limited resource is based on a logic of lack, the maintenance of which is instrumental in sustaining social inequities. Fame, or social capital, provides the artist access, support and encouragement, which the artist feeds back into the system, creating more opportunities for connections to occur.

While social capital is an important force and something that the civically engaged artist should work to manufacture, mobilize and enjoy, a girl's still gotta pay the rent, and it's hard to exchange coverage in the entertainment weeklies for a place to sleep. And, ultimately, it's tough to argue that a little scratch doesn't do a lot to advance any cause. So, where can the artist as civic engager find resources, particularly considering the lack of widespread interest in strongly supporting public arts funding? In neo-liberal theory, the erosion of the public sector was intended to give the private sector an opportunity to step in and get involved. Government facilitated this by making it easier to set up foundations, allowing individuals and companies with fewer resources to act collectively. This has yielded a proliferation of individual and corporate foundations often established through a rhetoric of social responsibility and good corporate citizenship.

One such institution is the Laidlaw Foundation, based in Toronto. Established in 1949, the foundation focuses on three spheres: the environment, children and youth, and the performing arts. Recently, after a round of soul-searching, the foundation is adding a screen to its arts funding by requiring that applicants must create work 'of, by, with or for excluded youth,' by which it means poor youth and youth of colour. This tendency for foundations to focus on youth is widespread but is of particular interest in the case of the Laidlaw Foundation because it publicly identifies as left; it's not simply out of rational do-gooderism that it's making this shift, but because it's trying to shape socio-economic conditions in a particular direction. In the eighties this desire for change saw the Laidlaw Foundation narrow the criteria for eligibility in the performing arts to original Canadian scripts, scores and choreography – funding was available only to strictly homegrown projects. In this way, the foundation was instrumental in creating a causeway for the incredible burst of creativity during that decade, including a proliferation of development festivals and small production companies.

But this is no longer enough. Denis Lefebvre, the foundation's Arts Program Manager, in a series of consultations with stakeholders, has expressed frustration with the amount of work the foundation is funding that is insufficiently engaged with its mission to promote progressive change. Some of these artists argue for the conception of the artist as one who – for the edification of all – is allowed to follow her whims, no matter where that may take her. But that's a conception of the artist Laidlaw doesn't seem to share as it lowers the screen of 'excluded youth' in front of its programs. The foundation is abandoning the idea of privileging craftsmanship, a universal ideal of beauty and the material art object, and instead looking toward process and direct engagement with the social, political and economic spheres.

So what the fuck is this, the artist resplendent in his rigour wants to know – *social work?* The artist is being asked to adapt, to consider other populations, fields and relationships as both collaborators and artistic material. But once the socially engaged artist understands that particular populations and relationships are potential material, the funding opportunities open up even beyond the arts-focused foundations. Many other foundations, while cool to art, are keen to work with individuals working with at-risk and underserviced populations. For the artist willing to engage with these populations and situations, there's the opportunity for resources. And for the activist, there's art as a vehicle for projects that otherwise might attract unwanted resistance or not generate the same interest as traditional social work.

In terms of the private sector, I want to touch briefly on the Toronto phenomenon of two boutique hotels, the Gladstone and the Drake, both of which make claims – accurately or not – to social engagement. Jeff Stober, the owner of the Drake, states on the hotel's website that his aspiration is 'to create a democratic hub' and a 'cultural community centre.'[23] The Gladstone website states that their 'most important goal ... was to establish and maintain accessibility to art, community and culture.'[24] Obviously, any advertising rhetoric will exceed deeds, and certainly – as many have argued, particularly against the Drake – there's a chance that all this talk is masking a desire simply to create a party playhouse for the culturati. But this rhetoric is an invitation to push the boundaries of the offer. Such initiatives should not be accepted uncritically, but neither should they be dismissed out of hand. They should instead be tested; their limits should be consciously explored with an eye to these venues becoming further material to be deployed in creating engagement. This is a new kind of rhetoric issuing from a sector that has never made community-building a business venture. The idea of the artist-run venue with a café and full community engagement has fuelled the fantasies of places like Symptom Hall, the Theatre Centre and Buddies in Bad Times Theatre. With the neo-liberal turn, these visions had to be adjusted and scaled down; the hip alternative cultural community centre, complete with café, remains elusive – unless you take the stated goals of the Drake and the Gladstone at face value.

And, in the case of the Gladstone, why shouldn't we? The Zeidler family and their company, Urban Space, which owns and operates 401 Richmond and the 215 Centre for Social Innovation,[25] has managed to foster a civically engaged model of entrepreneurship, doing what the private sector was *supposed to do*, according to so much of the hot air of neo-liberal theory. That most of the privatization hasn't led to these kinds of initiatives should take nothing away from the fact that Urban Space has managed to make it happen. And be clear: I'm not arguing that the redistribution of wealth upwards that has followed neo-liberal reforms is something we should not oppose. But there are wealthy individuals and organizations who can be considered allies or whose resources can be accessed and utilized, to some degree, in efforts to re-redistribute.

The jury is still out on how Stober and the Drake will fare, but it's interesting to note their website recently underwent a subtle but important upgrade when the pronouns were shifted from Stober's 'I' to a more inclusive 'we.' Window-dressing? Maybe. But the newness of these projects should be taken into account. They both claim to be open to community input. It's the responsibility of the community to put this invitation to a rigorous test. And if they don't walk their talk, *then* we'll burn them to the ground.

NEO-PHILISTINISM, NEO-BOHEMIANISM AND THE SOCIAL IMPRESARIO

Perhaps our thinking needs a new approach to philistinism, one that considers art from a very critical – if not skeptical – angle. The term 'philistine' usually refers to middle-class people indifferent or antagonistic to artistic and cultural values, preferring material enhancement. The term contrasts with bohemianism, which traditionally evokes individuals uninterested in the material, preferring a care-free, roving lifestyle of detachment. But currently, we see a new kind of bohemianism intentionally practiced by horny capital in places of speedy gentrification like Brooklyn's Williamsburg and Toronto's Queen West. This leaves us the possibility of a neo-philistinism that sits in opposition to this neo-bohemianism. As with old philistines, there remains a suspicion of artistic endeavours that don't engage with the material, specifically the material of the viewer's body – and a privileging of work that accumulates capital, but not just any capital: social capital. Neo-bohemianism, on the other hand, would describe a hypocritical affectation of a commitment to a non-material, more carefree approach to life, in a vain (pun intended) attempt to mask a desperate and nasty elitism and classism. James Vision, programmer at De Leon White Gallery, in an interview with *Diplomatic Immunities* and while wearing a shirt emblazoned with the word 'bohemian,' displays this kind of headspace as he talks excitedly about social cleansing: 'The changes [along Queen West] create an environment that cuts out that street-level class of individuals. It's a whole different crowd coming down to the area: people with money, people that are responsible with direction in their life.'[26]

There's an urgent need for those of us interested in addressing global inequities to spend the time envisioning and developing new social relations. Adopting a loose, flexible neo-philistinism that has a clear grasp of the constantly shifting strategic uses of art and culture could provide a compass to help us strategize in our own artistic practice and consumption. Avoiding art and artistic practices that don't directly and tangibly question the material differentials and how they play out in the global economic field would not be absolute, but the guide for a temporary strategy.

Perhaps, then, we have the possibility of the neo-philistinian artist as social impresario, a skeptical coordinator of unlikely or particularly charged encounters, working out of a selfish need to make her world a better place and masquerading as a do-gooder to generate support from both private and public sectors. When ambition and desire for a shit-hot career drive the artist to acts of social good, who cares that the motivations are less than pure? The funding (public and private) and support milieu (media, galleries, boutique hotels) can conspire to reward rigorous acts of progressive social engagement.

PART THREE
SOCIAL ACUPUNCTURE

Acupuncture is a mildly invasive modality that affects the chi, one of the body's fundamental substances, often translated into Western thinking as energy. This westernized conception insists on a distinction between form and function that is not present in Chinese medicine, where chi is more accurately understood as the functioning of the body's different systems as much as something that infuses those systems with life.

Ideally, chi flows smoothly, and all the body's systems along with it, but it can also be clogged, creating an excess, or it can be deficient, leaving the body depleted. If we think about chi in a social context, excess might be the presence of a coercive force, such as the state or other forms of authority, blocking healthy interactions, while a deficiency might be a situation without community links, networks or social capital.

This is a simplistic description; the social body, like the physical body, is a complex and nuanced system with many excesses here and deficiencies there. For example, the amount of resources plugged into the media spectacle, with its endless parade of entertainments, is an excess dialectically related to a deficient and apathetic, politically alienated public. And just as the physical body experiences energetic eddies and stagnations leading to chronic holding patterns, so, too, does the social body. In the physical body, a chronic holding pattern may develop due to tension in a given set of muscles: the shoulders creep up or the butt is clenched and the excess of nerve impulses in the area – the excess of energy – creates a tension that restricts the flow of blood and nutrients. Here, excess leads to a deficiency. Eventually, problems arise: pain, restricted mobility or worse. In the social body, an excess of power or opportunity held by one group – white people, for example – is contingent on a deficiency in other parts of the social body, and again we have pain, restricted mobility and worse. Classism, racism and sexism can all be read this way.

Traditional Chinese medicine is not as attached to first causes as its Western counterpart; there is no search for an underlying and definitive reason for disease. Instead, the whole body is seen in process, a system whose interlocking parts contribute to the situation in a continuous feedback loop. For example, there is no viral or bacterial theory, not because there wasn't the technology back in the day to detect the microbes, but because it doesn't matter – the streptococcus bacteria in your throat are always there, but they only become a problem when your immunity is compromised. There's no need to identify bacteria as the first cause, as there is in Western medicine, since the bacteria matters only in certain circumstances – circumstances that can be avoided through a preventative and holistic approach to health care. That's not to say antibiotic herbs don't exist, but they just don't play the central role they do in Western medicine.

Acupuncture is used to break system-wide holding patterns that are compromising the function of nervous, muscular, vascular, organ and psychological systems – these never viewed separately but always as a totality. And just as chains or archipelagos of tension link psyche and soma across disparate parts of the body, the elements of the social body are intertwined. The lack of free public space for unstructured discourse can be seen both as symptomatic of a democratic deficiency and as contributing to the situation, in what amounts to a feedback loop, each contributing to deterioration of the other. In the physical body, eddies of energy can gather far from the problematic area – the bottom of the foot is connected to the healthy functioning of the kidney, for example. Needling distant muscles can affect organs, and the whole system responds to the intervention. It shouldn't be surprising that the organs affect the muscles and the muscles affect the organs, that both affect the emotions, and that no single aspect of the entire system should be isolated and analyzed without taking the whole into account. Theoretically, then, the same thing should apply to the social body: small interventions at key junctures should affect larger organs, in turn contributing to feedback loops that can amplify and affect the distribution of energy resources.

THE SOCIAL ACUPUNCTURE OF
MAMMALIAN DIVING REFLEX

Much of the work outlined below was conducted under the auspices of Mammalian Diving Reflex, a collaboration between myself and producer Naomi Campbell. The company's Social Acupuncture wing was initiated in response to the waning cultural significance of theatre as well as a frustration with the formal conventions of theatre, including representation, character and acting. I wanted my work to affect the world, touch people's lives directly and contribute to a healthy functioning social sphere. To tell intricate representational stories of love, death and loss, trying to express some universal sentiment, more and more seems an act of complicity with a depressing status quo. But the paradox of political art, at this time in history, is that, for the most part – and excepting some of the more gruesome details – everybody pretty much already knows the scoop. Or, at least, everybody who's going to drop in on one of my shitty little plays already knows. Or, at least, they will claim to know, rendering any efforts to affect consciousness useless. People will be grateful for my efforts to speak politically, not because I'm making any dents in the way things are but because those fellow travellers are relieved to hear someone say it onstage. But while providing a little entertainment for the converted does give some satisfaction, that satisfaction doesn't tend to linger. Instead, social acupuncture offers the opportunity to directly engage with social flows, applying the same principles as real acupuncture, only the terrain is the social body instead of the physical body.

Like real acupuncture, social acupuncture can be uncomfortable, but this is a good thing. The dispersal of holding patterns, of energetic excesses and deficiencies, will usually generate discomfort, the social equivalent of confusion, a necessary part of any learning process. The feeling of the needles during acupuncture can vary. It can just plain hurt, like you'd expect of any needle. But more often the sensations are of a whole other order; the needle can feel heavy and almost nauseating at the point of entry; it can feel electric, the sensation travelling the length of the nerve; it can feel kind of itchy. It can also reproduce the sensation you're trying to eliminate by getting acupuncture in the first place, just like a shoulder massage can initially hurt but lead to a more relaxed state.

Analogous sensations and effects are felt with social acupuncture. The social awkwardness and tension it generates can feel stupid, the projects seeming to constantly teeter on the brink of embarrassment and failure. As any system experiences a shift into higher complexity, there will be a time when it feels like there has been a drop in understanding, dexterity or control. For example, in the traditional play-development process, there is the moment when the writer hands the script to the actors and has to endure their first awkward sweep through the work. Once the group gains an understanding of the movement of the piece, things begin to look good again, until it comes time get the show on its feet, at which point things feel bad again. This passes, things get smooth, and then it's time to add technical components, another layer of complexity that yields yet another wobbly and awkward transition where things feel stupid. The same is true with this work in the social sphere.

I should note that this work is the first attempt in this realm and can be considered a good start, but there's still lots to do. Like the other projects I mentioned earlier, I believe I can go further, engage with more challenging situations and make more interesting things happen. Please consider the work described here a first pass at something that will, I hope, become more sophisticated and effective with time. This writing represents my initial thoughts and findings on the subject after having conducted a series of preliminary social acupuncture experiments.

The focus of most of Mammalian Diving Reflex's social acupuncture is public discourse – talking between strangers in the public realm – because of my belief that it has potential to affect other systems. This is pure speculation, and hopeful – if not wishful – thinking. But on one occasion when the social circuits were disrupted through artificial means – the massive power outage of 2003 that crippled Ontario and a good portion of the American eastern seaboard – we saw an incredible surge of public generosity, connectivity and chit-chat. People, freed from the power – in both senses of the word – were jettisoned from their familiar social circuits, and social hierarchies wobbled, affording a glimpse at anarchism.

Here's the question: if a collapse in power yielded unfettered public discourse once, then could triggering unfettered public discourse do anything at all toward shifting the flows of patterns of power? Like I said, it's something that needs to be filed under wishful thinking. It's impossible to quantify, and its effects will be felt only over a significant period of time and with repeated applications – like any acupuncture.

THE TALKING CREATURE

The Talking Creature was the inaugural Social Acupuncture event, conceived in response to the 2003 Summer of SARS, when Toronto finally experienced a moment as the world-class city it had always wished it was – and it was quarantined.

It seemed that during this summer of civic isolation, anyone with enough wealth did their best to get out of town, leaving us poor people behind, creating an opportunity to establish connections and foster networks among those stuck in the city. It was paranoid thinking, but perhaps on some subtle level the makeup of the city was different that summer. I designed little flyers to hand around: 'The Summer of SARS is coming. The RICH will do their best to be out of town, leaving just the POOR. It might be a good time to do a lot of TALKING.'

The Talking Creature occurred five times during the summer and fall of 2003 in Toronto's Kensington Market, the Power Plant Art Gallery and the Peterborough Folk Festival under the auspices of Artspace, an artist-run centre. It was simple: a call for participants was made via email, in newsletters and, in the case of the Power Plant, an ad in *NOW* magazine. The text stated: '*The Talking Creature* is a participatory event examining the art of conversing with strangers in public. *The Talking Creature* examines this anxious dynamic in an ordered but random fashion, with the conviction that unfettered and fearless conversation between strangers is fundamental to freedom.' Participants would gather at a predetermined time and place and then disperse to scour the surrounding neighbourhood, approaching strangers and inviting them back to the meeting place for an unstructured, unagendaed conversation.

Part of the impulse behind *The Talking Creature* was a fatigue with the acceptable parameters for socializing. There is a lack of common space and few ways to hook up with new people outside the rigid conventions of bars, galleries, theatre lobbies and dinner parties – scenes generally requiring alcohol and a particular kind of wit where discussion surfs from one cultural meme to another. This kind of socializing has a value, but only within specific, arguably narrow, limits. There are few forums to meet people where identity and power dynamics do not dictate the parameters of discourse.

There were two remarkable aspects of *The Talking Creature*. The first was that the strangers approached were, for the most part, completely open and excited by the idea. There was almost no fear – a bit of confusion maybe, and the occasional inquiry about whether this was a religious thing. But most people were totally game. The second remarkable aspect was the difference between the vibe before and after the search for strangers. Before, as the participants, most of whom did not know each other, stood around waiting for the event to begin, there was palpable tension; no one knew what to do or say. We were about to do something that, according to the great myth of liberal democracy, should be a comfortable given, but in reality it's horribly nerve-racking, throwing into question the very idea that we live in a democracy. If this place is so democratic, why can't strangers talk freely? Why is it often so onerous?

With *The Talking Creature* the context is neutral – we weren't there to talk about anything in particular, just to talk. Talking without an agenda among strangers is a rare thing. The only experience of talking to strangers that we regularly have is when they are serving us or we are serving them – the service industry the only field providing consistent encounters between people who don't have anything explicitly in common. So, nervousness prevailed at the onset of the experience. But once the strangers had been lured back, there was absolutely no need to facilitate the conversation, no need to provide a topic or structure. In fact, the conversation sparkled, almost manic in its urgency. The catalyst was the act of risk-taking; the energy invested in approaching strangers, or, in turn, trusting the stranger who had approached you, provided the forceful dividend of a surprising ease. The shared experience of talking to a stranger was the starting point, but that point was, more often than not, left far behind. No one stood around talking about talking. There were too many other pressing things on our minds.

That there is a latent and strong desire to experience the Other couldn't have been driven home more clearly than on August 14, 2003, when the blackout shut down Toronto and New York City, the former famous for the coldness of its population and the latter for their rudeness. But, dislodged from routine, many people became nearly ecstatic at the opportunity of communing with strangers, interacting with an openness and urgency remarkable for its relaxation, trust and joy: *The Talking Creature* as presented by the aging power grid and the miracle of privatization.

A SUICIDE-SITE GUIDE TO THE CITY

To return to the theatre from this experience is difficult, but I was charged with the desire to inject it with the kind of energy that occurred during *The Talking Creature*. I applied some of the principles to a solo show, *A Suicide-Site Guide to the City* (the text follows this essay), a collage of autobiography, fiction, confession and audience participation. Before the show, I hover in the lobby and try to introduce myself to every single audience member. I start the conversation by explaining that

I am the writer and performer of the show and asking what has brought them to the theatre. I usually follow this up by asking if they're involved in show business and, if not, what they do to raise their rent. If someone gets into the theatre before I can talk to them, I enter the house and sit beside them, initiating the same conversation.

I was surprised to discover that the audience appreciates the contact – some seem to be honoured by it – and that an easy rapport is quickly established. The atmosphere generated has a direct impact on the vibe in the room, making people willing to respond to me during the course of the show, with little effort required to get them to sing 'Happy Birthday' to my sister, who I claim is in the audience, and to join me onstage for a make-out session. It's important to note that, while mingling in the lobby, I am not 'in character'; there is nothing performative about what I'm doing, and when I'm asked if the conversations are a 'part of the show,' I say no, I just want to meet the people in the audience, which is true and not true. But the need to divide the experience into 'part of the show'/'not part of the show' reveals the desire to keep art locked securely in a category that is 'not life.'

The muscles developed through *The Talking Creature* are instrumental in creating the ease with which I am able to approach the audience and leads directly to establishing an open, communicative atmosphere. I realize I am conflating the problems of dramaturgy with those of performance, but, in my mind, a dramaturgy that does not take into account performance and audience does so at its own and the text's peril. How I anticipate the interaction with the audience has a direct effect on what and how I write. A writer who focuses strictly on the contours of her characters and their interaction, without taking into account that the audience is yet another character and an area where she will be projecting bits of herself, is missing a rich arena for an additional layer of drama.

A Suicide-Site Guide to the City incorporated the insights of *The Talking Creature* in a cautious and tentative way, testing the waters to see what kind of effect would be generated and if the experiment warranted more attention.

THE WALKING TALKING CREATURE

The Walking Talking Creature is a variation of *The Talking Creature* adapted to work with the Art Gallery of Ontario's Youth Council and the students of Parkdale Collegiate in Toronto. Unlike in the adult version of the event, I couldn't ask the youth to walk the city streets, approaching strangers and inviting them back for a casual conversation. Not that it would have been dangerous – downtown Toronto is a safe place and I trust that a bunch of seventeen-year-olds would know how to handle themselves. But it was a no-go from the point of view of the institutions, which, unsurprisingly, use the rhetoric of safety to cloak control. That we so easily accept that we can't promote talking to random strangers is a capitulation to unreasonable fears. In any case, the compromise was to take the entire class out onto the streets and, together, approach and talk to strangers. Because there were so many students and only one subject at a time, a dialogue didn't seem possible, so I informed the youth that they were allowed to ask any question they wanted, no matter how intrusive, ridiculous, inappropriate or disrespectful, knowing that the kids would remain within the bounds of propriety; in the unlikely event they didn't, I informed the subjects that it was their responsibility to draw the line – they didn't have to answer any questions they didn't want to. This principle has become central to all such interview work and, while it may seem self-evident, more than once the subject had to be reminded of his or her inherent right of refusal. It appears that the pressure exerted by a bunch of students can be hard to resist.

One of the reoccurring things I've noticed while creating this work is the simultaneous insistence on protecting individual human rights and the complete disavowal of any kind of discomfort. In its more progressive manifestations, this results in people insisting on spaces of safety where no one runs the risk of being triggered. Often, though, unease about discomfort and the neurotic desire to make sure everybody feels good hide a fearful controlling impulse, leading to atomized enclaves where difference is rejected and communities are comfortable only with people who look and think like themselves. Obviously, this is something we see with more conservative folks, bent on keeping difference at bay, but I also find this in so-called progressive communities where personal comfort takes precedence over movement building. Again, there's little doubt that such manoeuvres have their place – organizations need caucuses to protect the rights of minority groups – but it's a fine line between creating a safe space for particular people and rejecting uncomfortable difference in favour of homogeneous blobs of people who trust each other. Social discomfort is analogous to cognitive confusion: when you're learning something new, you have to accept that you will spend some time in confusion, and when you're increasing your social intelligence, you will spend some time in discomfort.

In Parkdale, the group of thirty students, as well as teachers Marie Axler and Tina Cervin-Shaw, walked around the neighbourhood, the students often recoiling from contact with a whole range of people: the eldery, the sketchy, the preoccupied, people who appeared busy, grumpy, etc.; the students' prejudices became undeniably material as they scurried out of the path of anyone who made them feel uncomfortable. I would call the students on their irrational fears and force an interaction. People usually agreed to our request, openly talking to the students, many regarding the participation as a communitarian act and giving generously of their time and the details of their life.

Not only is *The Walking Talking Creature* instructive about unconsciously held prejudices about other people, it can also address other prejudices, like those about a given space. We met Cliff Allen, who told us he was a country singer recently signed to Sony, and he had just messed up the lyrics to 'O Canada' at a Blue Jays game. Though they withheld their comments until the debriefing, a lot of the students didn't believe the guy. I returned with a newspaper article about the incident, but still many of the students insisted he was lying, that it must have been someone else who had screwed up the national anthem. This, to me, seemed preposterous, but for the students it was more preposterous that people who get signed to Sony and sing songs at baseball games live in their own neighbourhood. Their assumptions about Parkdale – that there was no one there who had accomplished anything of any note – proved to be not so, and the students had to either resist or revise their assumptions. Most resisted, some revised.

In Parkdale, the youth inevitably wanted to know how the adult subjects felt about the neighbourhood's safety, because Parkdale's mythology, with its mix of poor white people, folks with mental-health issues and recent immigrants, is one of danger. It's a story the students hear from authority figures all the time, but once we accept that stray gunshots, while they do occur, are less of a threat than stray bathtub slips, the neighbourhood becomes dangerous only under specific circumstances. Of course, this doesn't take into account the danger emanating from the state and its racist/classist policing, which *The Walking Talking Creature* wasn't able to do anything about. Addressing the neighbourhood's self-perception, however, was possible. The youth heard again and again from the various subjects that their neighbourhood was a safe place.

While performing *The Walking Talking Creature*, I was surprised at how comfortable people were while chatting with a bunch of teenagers. The students were sensitive to any discomfort the subject was feeling, experiencing it empathetically and managing to keep the ball rolling smoothly in what usually ended up more of a spontaneous conversation than an interview. The intriguingness of this social suaveness, combined with the fact that it was extremely entertaining, led Naomi and me to isolate this dynamic, calling it Q&A and trying it out in a more formal theatrical context, first as a late-night performance during Buddies in Bad Times Theatre's 2005 Rhubarb! Festival and again at Buddies during a dedicated night in Tallulah's Cabaret.

As the audience entered the theatre, they were asked to write their names on pieces of paper. During the performance, we drew names and brought individual audience members onstage, inviting the rest of the audience to ask them questions for five minutes. There were a few rules: to gain admission to the theatre you had to submit your name, but, if called, you had no obligation to participate – but you had to state this publicly. Also, the audience could ask the subject any questions they wanted, but the subject had no obligation to answer.

This licence to say no emphasized the responsibility and power of the subject. This might, at first, appear self-evident, but in the heat of the moment and with the strange power dynamic generated in the room, there's a concern that things can go awry – someone unwittingly blurting out something they may regret. But, regret it or not, the subject must take full responsibility. No one can else can say no for him or her; if the subject is cornered with improper questions, there's no need to get wound up – he or she just has to say no. This is a very personal point for me, suffering as I do from a compulsion to ask things I'm not supposed to ask – something Tourette's-like in its visceral insistence. Keeping my mouth shut leads first to an accumulation of manic energy and the desire to wildly misbehave, followed by fatigue, ennui and depression. I believe in the inherent right to ask prying and inappropriate questions, as long as the right of refusal accompanies it. I hope that, more than defending my right to be a jerk, this kind of thinking provides a way to accept responsibility for our own interactions. Again, this relates to my suspicion that in the drive toward the liberal universalist notion of human rights that characterized the last fifty or so years, there has been an accompanying oversensitivity that, in practice, keeps us atom-ized and more likely to be manipulated and have our rights impinged upon.

Beyond the simple but direct demonstration of self-responsibility, Q&A accomplishes another level of social acupuncture by proving that the banal minutiae of other people's lives can be as compelling and entertaining as any carefully constructed performance. In the arena of artifice, the unscripted and accidental is often much more beautiful, astonishing and revealing than the rehearsed. But getting someone onstage to simply be, without performing, has always been one of theatre's most daunting aspirations. In this society of extras, the expectation that life will provide momentous meaning often leaves disappointment and boredom in its wake. Most forms of entertainment, perhaps especially those that claim to provoke thought, offer us representations of life filled with non-stop action, love, longing, loss and significant historic events. For the most part, though, daily life is boring and hardly worthy of traditional approaches to drama; even if I were stuck in a consumerist nightmare (I am), an American jail (I'm not) or immersed in some future sudden shift of economic relations (I wish), a lot of my time will be spent between events, waiting, planning and hoping for something to happen. If I can't give this waiting the same kind of validity our culture assigns to the big stuff, I have to reconcile myself to my life's invalidity – something I'm not interested in doing.

'Surveillance' is observation from above, from the French 'sur,' while 'souveillance,' a word coined by cyborg Steve Mann,[27] describes the process of turning the cameras around and pointing them up from below at authority. Social acupuncture might be described as 'entreveillance,' observation from between or within, the scrutiny of one another within a dynamic of relatively evenly distributed power, where the observed can walk away from the camera at any point and the interest is in observing the quotidian rather than anything spectacular. When talking honestly about ourselves is the goal of a spectacle, the spectacle loses its power as such, and we are the only thing left. It feels good to sit in a room with a bunch of people and reconnect with the basic principles of inquiry and self-responsibility. These first principles cannot be assumed. There are rare situations where there is licence to inquire to one's heart's content and there are plenty of times when we have to answer questions against our will. In Q&A, we are stripped of prohibitions on both sides of the equation: we're free to ask anything and free to answer nothing. This is a powerful dynamic, one that generates an openness and sense of community where the audience is left feeling that they lived something as opposed to having merely watched it.

Q&A IN THE CLASSROOM

After doing q&a in the theatre, I took it to students at Malvern and Lakeshore Collegiate high schools. Instead of working in the surrounding neighbourhood, we remained in the classroom and hallways, with the students interviewing each other. Relatively meaningless interaction with only curiosity as a motivating force gave the students an opportunity to get to know each other outside of entrenched identity dynamics. Dances, sports and clubs offer social opportunities, but only as a contingency and only through predetermined identities and social groups. The purely social – if there is such a thing – is rarely addressed, the interaction of the multitude in the commons now wiped out of collective experience. One of the students, a girl who had immigrated from India a couple of years earlier, described this problem, noting that she missed the random neighbourhood conviviality that happens in India. She pointed out that, in Canada, social engagement always occurs through consumer activities like movies, drinks or shopping, while in India people tend to socialize by helping each other.

As a group we wandered the halls, looking for students who were not in class. We cornered them and subjected them to our gentle interrogation. I expected resistance to this, thinking we would be turned down by shy students unwilling to submit to the strange situation. Surprisingly, we had no difficulty finding students willing to be interviewed; the reluctant subject was the exception. Word quickly travelled through the school, and students began calling out, requesting interviews. The ambiguous difficulty of socializing was stripped

away; the awkwardness was concentrated and accepted, so no one really paid it any mind. Instead, most students – even the shyest – responded with wit, charm and charisma. It was okay to be frightened in this forum because everyone was frightened: the interviewers/students were frightened of silence and the subject was frightened of judgment. But the barrage of questions coming from a bunch of students diffused these problems; it wasn't a single tack of questioning from a single agenda. The students crowded around their peers, enjoying the freedom to inquire and their moment in the spotlight.

Ultimately, the reason the students had so much fun with this exercise is obvious: everybody loves attention. Attention, arguably, is fundamental to our health; if we're not receiving enough of it, we tend to behave in ways that generate it – negative attention often being better than none at all. Q&A provided the sensation, however briefly, that there was organized and systematic interest in the student and her views, an interest that was not attached to achievement, merit or success, nor was it punitive, coercive or controlling. It was an attention that was, in fact, almost meaningless. She wasn't being interviewed because she'd done something bad or something good, and her views would not be put to any use whatsoever. We were simply interested in the banal facts of her life because she is a worthy person.

The limits of this kind of open inquiry were tested in a collaboration with art collective UPBAG in a *Halloween Q&A*. We took over a room at the Gladstone Hotel and, as part of Canzine, a zine fair organized by *Broken Pencil* magazine, installed an apocalyptic cityscape with a video component that situated the subject in the middle of all the destruction. The same rules applied: I and anyone else in the room could ask the subject anything we wanted, though any question could be refused. It being Halloween, I wanted to ask people scary questions, granting myself full licence to break every rule of propriety with the expectation that people would take full responsibility for themselves. I may have taken the thing a little too far, asking if people had ever been sexually abused, ejaculated on/in without consent, whether they ever felt like killing anyone, whether they ever felt like killing themselves and on and on. Though not convinced the project could bear the full

weight of the metaphor, I was also trying to tacitly refer to the proliferation of interrogation in the post-9/11 world, hoping that, for the attentive, the reference might be worthwhile.

Interestingly, most people submitted without protest, answering most questions and rarely objecting. Afterwards, though, I received several angry emails. Again, this brings up the question of responsibility: the responsibility of the subjects for their own discomfort and the responsibility of the artist who has generated the situation. It also invites us to consider the general assumption that harm can be caused by simply asking inappropriate questions. The most common concern in the complaints was the inequitable power dynamic in the room – I'm a relatively straight white male – and the trauma the work could have caused had the subjects been people with lower thresholds, one email suggesting that suicide could be a potential outcome.

It's easy to speak of 'what ifs' but difficult to gauge their relevance. But maybe they're right. Maybe my belief that the *Halloween Q&A* questioned this very idea of power by creating a space where, in actual fact, all the power is in the hands of the subject, facing interrogators with no means or desire to force anyone to do anything they didn't feel like doing, was delusional. Was the project so powerful as to deprive people of the will to leave, forcing them to retreat into suicide? One concerned person felt a pressure to answer the questions, and to be 'cool' about it. Is it true that responsible and free adults can't be trusted to protect themselves from unwanted intrusions in the name of being cool? Since then, I've talked to a lot of people about the *Halloween Q&A*. There are strong opinions on both extremes, leaving me as confused as ever. In the end, I decided I would rather err on the side of prudence and stop the aggressive Q&As.

However, aggression is often in the eyes of the beholder, with small acts of social impropriety triggering paranoia. *Home Tours*, first tested in Toronto and then used as a research module for *Diplomatic Immunities*, is a simple project where we take a group of people around random neighbourhoods, knock on doors and request a quick look inside. In February 2006 we spent an afternoon walking around Calgary's wealthy Mount Royal neighbourhood. The reception was not warm; a couple of individuals contacted Alberta Theatre Projects, our host company, to complain about our lack of common sense and to suggest that they might take 'further action.' We were told, 'Receiving strangers at the door, uninvited, in the middle of the afternoon, would be scary to anyone.' It was a challenge for ATP to fully back us, as they had to be careful not to alienate their audience and donor base. We were asked to mitigate the real fear on the part of our respondents and to perhaps approach the houses in smaller groups of two.

Once again, a discomfort with discomfort proves to be something the subjects cannot accept. It didn't matter that we weren't actually a threat; what mattered was that some people feel threatened by anything deviating from the norm. The fact that discomfort is simply unacceptable speaks to the degree to which current social flows, networks and dynamics are entrenched and inculcated on both sides of the political spectrum (however weak and vague these designations may be): on the left, with human rights discourse, the need for safe space and the right not to be triggered, and on the right a defence of the sanctity of private property and the right to enjoy obscene largess undisturbed. Both positions are reluctant to weather discomfort, leaving many restrictive assumptions unquestioned.

The tension wasn't nearly so pronounced in the Toronto version of *Home Tours*, as we weren't examining class dynamics. In August 2005, as part of the Summerworks Festival, thirteen audience members and I checked out the houses surrounding the Factory Theatre, walking east along Adelaide Street. We were warmly welcomed into the home of a young nightclub promoter, a tiny two-bedroom apartment with a roommate, a cramped kitchen the only shared area. The whirlwind tour included the beer fridge in his bedroom, a few chin-ups on the bar in the doorway and some artwork created by local graffiti luminaries. Just down the street, a marriage counsellor working from home couldn't disrupt his session, but his wife agreeably hung out with us on their patio under a canopy of grape vines. Around the corner on Portland and Richmond, we toured a live-work architecture firm that was designing a new superjail for juveniles. The assistant gestured to drawings on the wall, self-consciously assuring us that the kids would have lots of green space to roam. Across Richmond was the live-work space of a couple of high-end graphic designers responsible for products like Cat Chow and Stouffer's frozen dinners. There is obviously money in that

field; their beautiful house had been repeatedly photographed and recently featured in the *Globe and Mail.* It was a stunning place, complete with a rooftop garden and a system to recycle rainwater.

In September 2005, eight of us walked north from the Bathurst subway station to explore the Annex, finding a little more reluctance and paranoia. With some persistence, we managed to tour the digs of a couple of newlyweds, a grad student and an English professor from the University of Toronto. We hung out in the prof's backyard and spent some time getting to know each other – the group of participants as strange to each other as to our various subjects. When we departed, the prof gave us full access to his herb garden, encouraging us to take home handfuls of pungent sage, oregano, rosemary and basil. The only conflict in that neighbourhood was with the woman who nervously turned down our request and demanded to know if we had stolen the herbs.

SPIN THE BOTTLE

It's one thing to induce conversation and questioning between strangers, even invade their homes, but it's another thing altogether to start to tinker, however playfully, with the world of sex. Though it can be argued that kissing is simply talking with fewer syllables – after all you do still have the give and take of moving lips, tongues and, if the kissing is really good, vocal cords. The social acupuncture undertaken to engage participants in playful explorations of more sexually charged intimacy wasn't intended to address sexuality as such but, rather, all the anxiety around in-crowds, coolness and self-esteem.

Spin the Bottle started during the summer of 2003, the summer of SARS, the summer of the blackout – the same summer as *The Talking Creature.* I remember this summer, as a time when certain community-building energies were released, like a puff of tonifying gas. It was a time when Toronto found a little of its identity both as a city in its own right and as a city imbricated in a different kind of global network, a network of plague and potential destruction and collapse; the city was an international pariah, but once it was quarantined with the lights dimmed, it was found to possess a wealth of latent generosity. With SARS, the connection to Asia proved something that had been true all along: our destiny is linked not only to Europe but to other continents too. On the ground, SARS had very little effect on Toronto, but on the level of spectacle, it was a really big show. I wonder if that summer may at some point be regarded as instrumental in a shift in civic consciousness; in any case, I'd like to contribute to that view, in that it fomented a shift in my consciousness. I hope it will be seen as a time that unleashed certain forces, like the single degree of heat that's added to water as it shifts from 99 degrees to 100, when things – while still water – look entirely different.

That summer I'd had enough of hearing myself drone on during various readings, so for Louise Bak's Box Salon at the Rivoli, I chose to play with the media image Toronto had been given as the place of plague and prove to the world – or at least to each other – that there was nothing to fear. So I thought a big game of *Spin the Bottle* would be just the thing. The room was filled to capacity, but I cleared a space in the centre and got the game rolling. As a first go, it was successful, in that people were good enough sports to play, but things remained chaste. It was still early in the evening, it wasn't a party and people weren't drunk. Artists Simone Moir and David Findlay did step up with their tongues and provide some scintillation, but for the most part it was sweet pecks on the cheek. One beautiful coincidence was a kiss that passed through a family, with a mother, father and daughter all finding the bottle pointing toward them in succession. Obviously, they kept their tongues under wraps.

That fall, the art collective Instant Coffee invited me to host a game during their Basement Makeout party at the bar Revival. It was an intimate night, with mostly friends and associates, but the desire to play the game was strong. This was not something I had expected: people were nervously coming up to me, like junkies, demanding to know when I was going to start spinning. The pun is good: I go to parties and spin, but not vinyl.

When I told a friend about the first *Spin the Bottle* performance, she responded negatively, citing teenage trauma as the source for her antipathy toward kissing games. Certainly, *Spin the Bottle* does tend to trigger sensitive memories for many people. Public smooching at teenage parties is a ridiculously difficult rite of passage. I was interested in creating relatively inclusive spaces where the dynamic would be introduced and if you had any desire to participate you simply had to step up. I know I'm indulging in utopianism. Of course there are barriers to participation – only certain people would have heard of the event, only certain people would feel comfortable enough to attend, etc. But for those who attended, the game was open to whoever wanted in.

Back of the Bus took this dynamic further, mixing it with that other common trauma: the cool kids partying at the back of the bus. Conceived to entice people to make the long trek up to the Art Gallery of York University's show *Sinbad and the Rented World*, *Back of the Bus* played with generating an in-crowd. When people stepped onto the bus, they were asked if they were interested in participating in a kissing game. Those who were wrote their name on a piece of paper. I invited the bus driver to play the game by drawing the first name out of the hat. The chosen one went to the back of the bus and pulled a name out of the hat and that person would join the first person at the back and they would kiss for a minute. Then they, in turn, picked a name and another person would join, forming a make-out chain. The parameters of the performance were selected so that I could keep everybody occupied for the entirety of the forty-five-minute trip. Over the course of the journey, the back of the bus was increasingly occupied by a loud, active make-out party, while the front was filled with people sitting silently, staring stiffly forward, their arms crossed on their chests.

Social acupuncture generates situations that trigger extreme reactions in a safe, controlled way, so the bus, with its ecstatic in-crowd making all the noise and having all the fun in the back, reproduced the same kind of teenage dynamic as *Spin the Bottle*. Over the course of the journey, about thirty people made their way to the back of the bus to engage in kissing and other hilarity – there was lots of yelling, laughter and fun. It created a clear divide between those who chose to participate and those who didn't. As the kissers began to occupy more and more of the back of the bus, the non-kissers were left in the front, unable to see what was going on, more and more hostile, forced to listen to all the fun the cool kids were having – just like the cool kids on all the various buses of our lives. In this case, the crucial difference was that everybody had been invited to participate, therefore everyone was responsible for their own positions in the social fabric of the bus.

Triggering teenage anxieties may seem like a heartless thing to do, but inducing such feelings once we're out of our teenage years – and have applied some analysis and understanding to the dynamics – is a good way to reveal personal shortcomings and fears in a forum without risk or wider ramifications. Better you examine your unresolved issues of belonging during a performance on a bus in the liminal world between Toronto and North York than during a more crucial moment when something is actually at stake. Ideally, this provides participants a chance to examine and reflect on their reactions, taking responsibility for their own feelings. In any case, the people in the front of the bus got quiet and grumpy while the people in the back got loud and stupid: social acupuncture at its most refined.

The notion of treating something as ridiculous as make-out games with an academic seriousness is at the core of social acupuncture. The proof that these seemingly stupid activities can yield tangible and progressive results is found in the fact that they can trigger feelings of confusion and alienation. As with a real acupuncture practice, you locate the spots to needle by feeling for tenderness and pain.

WHAT KIND OF PERSON IS THIS?

Implicit in all of this social acupuncture is the power of judgment, of judging others, of judging ourselves, and a conscious triggering of this activity with full awareness in order to isolate and diffuse the dynamic. *What Kind of Person Is This?* indulged in this unabashedly. It was a simple performance created in collaboration with Emily Hurson and Mariko Tamaki for a Theatre Centre event in May 2004. Public impropriety was induced by encouraging people to judge us, a favourite no-no in polite society. The three of us walked along Queen Street between John and Spadina, approaching random strangers and asking them to tell us what kind of people they thought we were, inviting as many assumptions as they could muster. We recorded their comments and edited them down to the highlights. In performance, we played the audio while describing the people and sharing our assumptions about them. We finished the piece with the audio of a guy who had described us as 'perfect' since we had somehow managed to structure our lives in such a way that we could be wandering around on a warm spring afternoon asking people what they thought of us. He had given us his card, so we concluded the performance by calling him and getting the audience to shout out that he, too, was 'perfect.' *What Kind of Person Is This?* acknowledged the fact that assumptions are the grease that keeps social wheels rolling, providing both entertainment and a social service.

DIPLOMATIC IMMUNITY

This use of other people as material and the representation of others without affording them the ability to intervene or comment is an area of intense interest. *Diplomatic Immunity* was a simple piece about communication and the representation and telling of other people's stories. The initial inspiration was the problem of trying to engage artistically with political situations out of the realm of personal experience. The question of appropriation is important, presenting a frustrating paradox when one tries to create art that addresses social ills and engages with the concerns of under-represented communities.

As a white person, it can be tricky – there's a desire to include other points of view but also a reluctance to tell others' stories for them. I sidestepped this issue in my play *White Mice* by talking about systemic racism in Canada not from the point of view of a person of colour but from that of two white individuals whose consciousnesses were being shaped by of-colour individuals not represented onstage. Again, I dodged it with *pppeeeaaacceee* – not so nimbly this time – by creating a post-revolutionary, almost post-racial world, where awareness of difference had pretty much been eradicated; it was a prob-lematic world, no doubt, and, as such, an ambiguous but ulti-mately dystopian vision.

The real way through the impasse for people in my posi-tion is to focus on creating opportunities for collaborations where I'm not the only author/director in the process, where the power is shared and people can tell their own stories. This is still an uncomfortable compromise, as I sometimes want to tell stories all by myself and to feature characters who are not white. It's important to engage with stories and subjective positions that are far beyond lived experience as a way of devel-oping understanding and empathy. It's depressingly defeatist to give up and write only what one knows, rather than work-ing hard to stretch our imaginative capacities to wrap our minds around the conditions of others. That said, however, you have to be cautious, because the tendency toward oppor-tunism is always lurking.

Diplomatic Immunity was part of Theatre Columbus's 2003 Mayhem Festival, a biannual event focused on the first moments of the creative process. With *Diplomatic Immunity* I was looking to try new things both in form and content, and I also wanted to innovate in the realm of casting, to see if the randomness and anonymity of the Internet could break famil-iar patterns and induce unexpected relationships. I sent an email to the INCLUDE listserv, a community service started by writer/actor Bobby Del Rio for artists interested in strengthening the presence of people of colour in the entertainment industries. (To join, email Bobby at contact@bobbydelrio.com.) Rather than going the traditional route of accepting resumés and photos, I described the project in a way that was self-screening: dry, academic and inhospitable to individuals interested in self-promotion – not that the list is particularly prone to that, but actors will be actors. My intention was to see if viable groups of performers could be assembled without the audition process and without rejecting anyone. As anyone who has ever participated in an audition knows, it's hurtful and humiliating: sitting in the waiting room with other actors, everybody checking and psyching each other out, and then, in the actual audition, having to generate enthusiastic behaviour even while being asked to do the most idiotic shit. The casting method was an experiment in seeing if the language of the call itself could create a screen that would let only like-minded people through. It seemed to work, generating a cast that included Koom Kankesan, Margaret Lamarre, Sunday Muse, Yvonne Ng, Marilo Nunez and Tanya Pillay.

One week before we presented, we rehearsed for three hours. Rehearsal consisted of each person showing a photograph of himself or herself in a particularly charged situation and telling a complicated backstory, fielding questions from the rest of the group. We then did a mock-up of the form but without the content we would be using the following week; instead, together we retold the events of 9/11 as if to a person who was unfamiliar with the attacks. I wanted to see if it was possible to generate the kind of buzz that happens when a group of people stumble over each other to collectively recall a story, especially when bits of that story have been either lost or transmuted in the winding corridors of memory.

For the performance, each person stood at centre stage while the rest of the group took two minutes to work together to retell the story – after having heard it only the one time a week earlier. The retelling occurred quickly, complete with people contradicting and correcting each other, elaborating and adding details – in the same way that any group of people retelling a story will get things wrong, iron out details, remember different aspects and present an amorphous gestalt of the story, audience understanding floating to the surface in fragments rather than as a cohesive narrative arc. This provided much more space for the audience's imagination; they had to make interpretive decisions, choosing what to believe, whom to take with a grain of salt and whom to trust. The stories drifted out as an achronological cloud, functioning more as a representation of the memory of the story than of the story itself. After all the stories had been told, we presented a slide show featuring the photos. This provided the conceptual anchor for the piece, giving the audience a way in and distilling the swirl of information they had just been subjected to into something tangible. Surprisingly, the effect was emotional, with audible gasps from the audience. People told me later how moved they were when they saw the photos, how something that had been a strange abstraction had concretized when the visual element was added.

Because the group was assembled randomly and the members were not, for the most part, known to each other before the first brief rehearsal, what the audience witnessed was a community assembling itself before their very eyes and with their participation. The encounter with and interpretation/representation/dissection of the Other is fundamental to the process of self-definition for any group, and *Diplomatic Immunity* triggered this by creating a consensual gossip session. The group shares with the audience its view of the individuals in the group while revealing bits about themselves through the particular details they happen to remember and retell. There's that moment in a new group of people when two or more split off and share their opinions about the others. This common and essential dynamic is at the core of *Diplomatic Immunity*, with the sharing of opinions occurring in full view of the audience while the subject of the discussion stands there, silent, listening to it all. This familiar social force, used to generate a meaningful encounter among the performers and with the audience, became a staple when the project began to expand and morph into *Diplomatic Immunities*, pulling into its orbit many of the other activities under the banner of social acupuncture.

THE TORONTO STRATEGY MEETINGS

While assembling and activating community in performance is of interest, I am also concerned with balancing the exploration of the insights yielded by social impropriety with less playful, more earnest and more direct civic engagement. Driving all of the social acupuncture work is the perhaps paranoid desire to build movements and communities that, when the time is right, can respond with an organized force against the inequities of current economic arrangements. The delusional notion that revolution is imminent has been the driving force behind many of these projects, and while teleological thinking may be detrimental and lead to injustices on a large scale, when it comes to small-scale projects, such thinking might be good to employ even if only as a target. *The Toronto Strategy Meetings* occurred Mondays at 9 a.m. from September to December 2004, during Project Toronto, Toronto Free Gallery's inaugural show. The meetings were open to anyone but were specifically targeted at freelancers who either worked from home or cobbled together a variety of workplaces, leaving them without a team to report to. These meetings were conceived in response to Michael Moore's observation that 'the right wing gets up early in the morning;

we sleep in. They've already done a lot of damage by the time we're rolling out of bed.'[28]

Participation ranged from four to twelve people, with three becoming regulars. Attendees included an environmental scientist, a painter, a sketch comedian, an academic, a few visual and performance artists, a government bureaucrat, some musicians, a dancer, a few theatre artists and some activists. The meetings consisted of reports to the group from each participant: a brief outline of the individual's current projects, what weaknesses or problems the person was having, what she hoped to do about it, and her plan for the week. The meetings lasted an hour or so, with the time divided evenly and strictly between all participants. The meetings appealed to those who understand the value of self-responsibility as a social act and the power of the social sphere as a catalyst for personal aspirations. They were specifically scheduled during the first hours of the workweek to attract people keen to get rolling and to motivate those who tend to let things slide.

For me, the meetings were a success and helped spur the revelation – in tandem with all the Creative Cities hype – that artistic production is hard work, and to get anything of value done, you've got to treat it like the job it is. I found this a consolation, as it explained why so often it's just no fun. This, then, became a position from which to respond and resist, or at least demand greater participation in the affairs of the world.

MY LIFE IS A CONFERENCE

The realization that art is work, and not just any work but work that can easily consume all hours of the day, inspired *My Life Is a Conference*, a personal performance that invited discussion about the role of culture in the city and my – and other cultural workers' – role in keeping the wheels rolling. I was interested in critiquing the tendency of cultural workers to proudly let their labour breach any notion of a forty-hour workweek and spill into all hours and all areas of life. For a few weeks, I walked around with a name tag around my neck, explaining to people that since every encounter, every event, every social opportunity contains an opportunity to work, to network, to absorb, to synthesize and to produce, then my life must be a conference. As the charm of being a working artist has begun to fade and the reality of the situation to dawn on me, I noticed that Bourriaud's definition of the artist as simply a manipulator of signs was not only true but a vocation that could occupy every moment.

Art's drift out of the field of representation and its move into relational forms, as well as the ever-increasing economic expediency of culture in the so-called creative economies described by Florida and others, have created a proliferation of avenues through which to distribute artistry. The Situationists may have had some fantasies about the liberating potential of art as an everyday lived experience, where all moments of one's life become a creative opportunity; now we have the concomitant penetration of every moment by the potential to create and, in turn, to work. Hardt and Negri point out that capitalism is always innovating in response to resistance against it.[29] The freeing of labour from the Fordist regime of the factory floor was imagined, at first, to be a positive movement, but capitalism easily incorporated these innovations. The idea of working from home was once an appealing notion, but now it brings with it the opportunity to never escape work, to field emails at all hours, to always be lured to the humming computer for just another minute or two of labour.

So making everyday life creative, which seems to be a sweet thing, with visions of all moments dedicated to liberating the artistic impulse, has played directly into capital's slippery ability to sweep things up and put them to work. The city becomes a place of constant culture, where the cultural workers are only barely compensated for their labour, if at all. Festivals proliferate, with many people working for honorariums, on spec or, worse, spending money on entrance fees, a pay-to-play model that seems to make sense to most artists who have been conditioned to believe that they should be grateful for any opportunity to show their wares. During Artsweek, the annual civic celebration, the administration of 401 Richmond called for performance artists to animate their building, offering them the opportunity to showcase their work 'for free.' The sad nature of this inadvertent hypocrisy at play is surpassed only by the unquestioning acceptance of artists, happy to be granted such a bargain.

During events like Artsweek, and in the civic-boosterism talk of the creative city, the grateful participation of the artist is taken for granted – artists are lucky to be able to contribute to the engine of the economy! Even in brilliant projects like *[murmur]*, where people's personal histories of the city are recorded and signs posted with a number to call to hear the stories, people are expected to contribute their labour for free, with the understanding that the city is made a better place for all.

But maybe that's okay, particularly in the case of projects like *[murmur]*, which involve direct civic engagement in the creation of something that builds community, as opposed to individual art objects meant simply for aesthetic edification. The feeling of self-exploitation is ameliorated when the tasks undertaken have a tangible benefit to others. The acupuncture model and the application of traditional Chinese medicine on the social body sustain this view. If efforts are applied to improve the flow of resources to distant areas of the social body, these can have system-wide positive effects. Artistic production for the sake of one's own career is initially exciting, until one begins to understand that all this work tends to benefit others who are higher on the economic scale. This can be seen clearly in a phenomenon like the Edinburgh Fringe Festival or a place like the Drake, where the abundance of artistic production draws an audience whose resources are more likely to be channelled toward alcohol than toward the performers. Artistic civic engagement, on the other hand, while not the best forum for generating money, does provide the possibility for creating a positive and tonifying social environment where the artist can find sustenance in the fact that his work is a direct intervention in the functioning of the civic sphere.

BEACHBALLS41+ALL

With *Beachballs41+All*, undertaken in association with the Catalyst Centre, the intervention is decisive but understated. An aesthetic of civic engagement begins to manifest more tangibly, with work that reached far outside even the atypical dynamics of strangers on the street to bridge gaps between children and adults, using play as a forum. It was a simple intervention that tried its best to pretend not to be an intervention. In the consideration of civil society as material, we can itemize the materials in this particular piece: Mammalian Diving Reflex (MDR)'s charitable status, Liz and Rennie's No Frills grocery store, the Alexandra Park outdoor swimming pool, a bunch of children, a bunch of culturati and 400 inflatable beach toys. Through MDR's charitable status, 400 inflatable pool toys were donated by Liz and Rennie's No Frills to Alexandra Pool's Wacky Fun Day. Then, again using the resources of MDR, a call was made for participants to come down to the pool early in the morning to donate air and lung power. About twenty people showed up to inflate 400 water toys for about 100 kids.

The intention was to create an encounter between two sets of people who have very little contact. The first was the artsy culture types who check out MDR's work: friends, colleagues

and acquaintances – mostly white and, while not rolling in dough, certainly in relatively confident possession of social and cultural capital. The group included artists, curators, editors, producers, programmers, funders, academics and one guy training to be a United Church minister. The other population was the kids who frequent the pool; they usually come from the lower half of wards 19 and 20 (Kensington Market, the Alexandra Park Housing Co-op and surrounding area) and comprise a variety of ethnicities with lower-than-average household incomes.[30] Getting these two groups together was motivated by a desire to create a small alliance between the two populations, to offer the adults an opportunity to act in the interest of the kids and to have the kids be beneficiaries of random generosity. The intervention was not so much about reversing an already existing power dynamic – though it did do that – but, rather, introducing a relatively new and different dynamic, if only for the duration of the day.

Another of *Beachballs41+All*'s aims was to demonstrate abundance – thus the decision to offer the toys en masse to the kids and not hand them out in an orderly way. With 400 toys available, all the kids could take home as many as they wanted. For most of us, moments of abundant resources and time are rare; we are used to 'lack' as both a coercive idea and an oppressive reality. Thus the objective was to introduce the sensation of abundance to prove that it's possible, it exists, it's just a matter of shuffling a few things around – distribution, as always, being the issue.

If not for this abundant excess, *Beachballs41+All* would have looked a lot like charity. In its excessiveness, the event began to bear the weight of metaphor, artistic intention and intervention – but an intervention where the artist is barely noticed, and instead of being a creator, is a conduit for already existing energies and resources, redirecting and tweaking them. This strategy leaves plenty of room to experience the event with or without criticality. It doesn't matter if the point isn't understood by participant, onlooker or audience – the roles here being completely muddled – since the experience is being lived.

As I mentioned previously, charity remains liberal do-goodery if it doesn't acknowledge and, in fact, encourage selfishness. It's not enough that charity might be the right thing to do, but that you do it because you know it will render your life better. As long as the recipient is seen to be the only one on the receiving end, we sustain charity as an act of discrimination and tend to reinforce or sustain inequalities. In the case of *Beachballs41+All*, the benefit accruing to all the adults was the opportunity to hang around and have some fun.

Another result of the event was that adults and children who did not know each other played together, breaking one of the most sacred rules of childhood. The prohibition against talking – let alone playing – with strangers is irrational; children are more likely to be molested or abused in their own home than by any playful adult on the street. There is a strong perception of the public sphere as a place of danger and atomization rather than safety and communication, and the lack of spontaneous play between strangers in public is one of the clearest indicators that public space is a sphere of intense, mostly internalized, surveillance. It feels odd to try to advance the idea that children benefit from playing with strange adults (and vice versa) – not because the idea is particularly outlandish, but because it isn't outlandish at all. It is a case of notions of security and safety once again cloaking social control.

In any case, pools are great places to cavort. The sheer physical challenges offered by a tank of water level the playing field. No matter how powerful the individual, when you're only wearing a swimsuit and are up to your neck in water, it's hard to control outcomes – you've got to go with the flow. While most spontaneous play is anarchic, playing in water introduces an element that ensures equality: almost everybody becomes a kid again and all parties have the potential to benefit from experiencing the effects of this equality. Play holds abundant possibilities for public intervention, and bringing together atypical playmates also holds the potential for examining typical and problematic power dynamics.

HAIRCUTS BY CHILDREN

If play doesn't do it for you, perhaps hairstyles can. *Haircuts by Children*, which at this writing is about to occur, is a whimsical relational performance that engages with the enfranchisement of children, trust in the younger generation and the thrills and chills of vanity. The project continues the exploration of an aesthetic of civic engagement, with the materials being a Grade 5-6 class, four hair salons around the city, the Milk International Children's Festival for the Arts and a brave, willing public. These are combined to create a performance that engages viscerally with the theme of trusting the

judgment of children. The event is being framed as a call to allow children into the political process. Absurd as this may seem, I believe it's completely irrational to bar children from full political participation both from the perspective of the child but also when we take into account the greater good. Excluding a huge segment of the population – a segment in the midst of forming attitudes that will shape their behaviour for the rest of their lives – is a narrow-minded act that limits our own possibilities as adults.

Throughout May 2006, MDR will be training a group of Grade 5-6 students at Parkdale Public School to cut hair and then providing free haircuts at four locations around Toronto. *Haircuts by Children* invites the contemplation of a very simple image: a child cutting an adult's hair. The impact this image has, the sense of absurdity it almost inevitably generates, is based on the false notion that kids should not be trusted. It's absurd to grant children power over you, but I don't think it should be. Children are valid citizens. As social acupuncture, *Haircuts by Children* brings together adults and children in a situation that reverses the typical power dynamic, leaving the adults at the kids' mercy.

As I write this, *Diplomatic Immunities* is working its way through the development process. The intention is to take many of these social acupuncture activities, most of which happen out in the world, and somehow bring them indoors – a notoriously tough thing to do. The problem with hauling this kind of thing into the black box of the theatre or the white cube of the gallery is that, by definition, it's impossible to take unmediated public space inside and subject it to the scrutiny of an audience. The encounters that happen around the city in a variety of locales are interesting for the very reason that they're not happening on the stage. To bring it all inside directly contradicts this essential attribute.

Cultural critic Brian Holmes refers to the 'law of visibility in interactive art,' in which he posits that 'the more communication there is, the less it's visible. ... In networked art, which in many cases is an enlarged, genuinely dematerialized conceptualism, the most interesting part is played out in the participation that the artistic concept makes possible; the reflections or traces of the interplay almost always prove disappointing. ... It quickly becomes an aestheticization of communication, which hides the real stakes by rendering them visible.'[31]

While Holmes's points are well-taken, he's talking not about the act of reproducing communicative acts in the theatre but specifically about documentation that ends up in the gallery, spending most of its time alone on the wall or on the screen without a human to interpret or continue the interaction. Theatre offers a venue for representing the various encounters with live performers, but we're still left with the question of how to bring the excitement of interacting out in the public onto the stage. One source of inspiration and a potential way through this impasse was the artist's talk –

a convention that doesn't exist in theatre. A visual artist chatting extemporaneously about her practice while shuffling through slides and fielding questions from the audience felt like an appropriate performative structure to apply to the variety of social acupuncture projects, creating something that would hover between documentation and discussion, with the addition of a few theatrical flourishes to satisfy the drama-heads in the house. In this way we could create something that, while unable to generate the same kind of encounter that happens on the street, could work with those experiences as material.

Another strong impulse was the desire to create a work that did not require memorized lines and the artificiality that inevitably produces. Memorizing lines is ridiculous work, requiring the same level of creativity as washing the dishes, while demanding absolutely undivided attention. I wanted to develop a form that could work with the spontaneous and unmemorized contribution of the performers without resorting to improv or pretending. This was motivated by the desire to create an entertainment event that was as close as possible to simply hanging out while still being able to justify charging admission. This may sound glib, but the impulse to somehow capture the spontaneity and liveness of real life is a common one. I wanted to create a context where a bunch of human animals could be as riveting and compelling as they truly are in as close as we could get to their unadulterated habitat.

The show is also an experiment meant to address the atomization of roles in most theatre productions; there's a disconnect between art, administration and technical that ends up generating suspicion and resentment. The tension between tech and art is particularly pronounced, exacerbated by a fiscally driven process that sequesters the creative side in the rehearsal studio. They work without set, light or sound and arrive suddenly in the theatre with only a week or so to incorporate tech at a breakneck speed, in a manner that doesn't acknowledge the integral role these aspects play. The artists often demand an unrealistic level of faith from a crew that has been virtually excluded from the decision-making process. This often leads to the familiar phenomenon of the tech sector exerting what little power and creativity it has by placing reactionary restrictions and limits on what the artsters are trying to do.

This atomization also extends into the producing end of things, where it's sustained by what appears to be common sense: artists often warning each other against working with administrative personnel who have creative aspirations. I was curious about developing a form that could incorporate an atypical skill set, wondering if the expertise of the administrative end of things could contribute directly to what was happening onstage. This goes back to a distaste and dislike for acting and pretense: I wanted to get some interesting, intelligent people onstage to see if we could assemble something compelling without resorting to the kind of virtuosity usually associated with a good performance. There's an unquestioned and widespread adulation of virtuosity in theatre to the exclusion of other aesthetics, aesthetics that view the focus on 'good acting' as part of a set of limitations keeping theatre locked in tired circuits.

With these principles guiding us, *Diplomatic Immunities* was conceived. Once a month throughout the fall of 2005, a group of collaborators, including Faisal Anwar, Naomi Campbell, Ulysses Castellanos, Misha Glouberman, Rebecca Picherack, Tanya Pillay, Beatriz Pizano, Vicki Stroich and myself, went out into the public and focused on different populations and geographies, gathering experiences, stories, still photos and video for a half-day, assembling for a half-day, then rehearsing and presenting on a third day. September was a general look at the neighbourhood of Parkdale; November featured Amanda Biber's Grade 5/6 class at Parkdale Public School. December focused on survival strategies for the holidays, using the Bloor-Danforth subway line as our location; and in January we spent four hours interviewing Tony Clement, a homeless man who asks for change outside the 7-Eleven at College and Lansdowne, and did a show about his world and our responses to it.

We use the various social acupuncture modules – *Q&A*, *The Talking Creature*, *The Walking Talking Creature*, *Home Tours* – to generate material, the driving question simply being 'What kind of person is this?' We try as much as possible to hold off on predetermining an agenda, leaving the responses of our subjects to collide with our own curiosities. And we consistently see a generosity and openness that perhaps speaks to the truth of the Warholian fifteen-minutes-of-fame dictum; people are ready for it, happy to divulge intimate and surprising details of their lives. There is often a moment in this work when the dynamic shifts and the area turns into something of an agora; the subject-interviewer format is abandoned and other subjects drift in, attracted by the action, until multiple conversations erupt about a multiplicity of topics. This provides the kind of community experience that the student referred to when she complained of Canada lacking public venues for social interaction.

Unfortunately, a major limitation of this work is that the dramatic import is much easier to locate in the encounters themselves than in their documentation; without deeper research and analysis, they tend to deflate when brought back to the theatre. One woman told us she had recently given birth by C-section to a child she didn't know she was carrying, going so far as to show us her scar; but it's a challenge to take this story – shared with almost no context or details – into the theatre and make it dramatically viable without any other narrative points.

The *Diplomatic Immunities* team members are not journalists. We drop ourselves into the public domain and try to create sudden, brief and meaningful encounters without the depth and detail usually demanded from a narrative. The limitation of this became clear when we spent a week interviewing people around Parkdale: folks living in the neighbourhood, students, gallery owners and businesspeople. After five days, we presented a half-baked live documentary on some aspects of gentrification, a deeply unsatisfying flirtation that left everybody frustrated. What became apparent was that – like the encounters on the street – live bodies encountering each other in view of a fully participatory audience generated the vitality of the show. As much as the people we met on the street seemed to be the subjects of the performance, the show really had to be about the people in the theatre at the time of the presentation: us onstage and the audience wrapped in the comfort of darkness. It had to be about our encounters with each other, sparked by the encounters that we brought in from the outside world. The interviews we do and the people we present to the audience provide a catalyst for what happens in the theatre – it cannot be simply reportage. Audience participation had always been a desirable element, but, in practice,

it became the crucial element: we're there to induce a real-time encounter with real people using the interviews with the public outside the theatre as a catalyst.

Michael Hardt and Antonio Negri, in their books *Empire* and *Multitude* describe a new kind of revolutionary or world-historic subjectivity they call 'the multitude,' a new way of thinking about ourselves in relation to the world. When it's working well, *Diplomatic Immunites* induces the experience of the multitude by examining the public sphere and reproduc-ing, conflating, collapsing and questioning the identity/difference dichotomy. It does this by creating self/other situa-tions that double back and swallow their own tails by generat-ing sympathy and antipathy at the same time. Tony, the home-less man, confounded our liberal expectations for a heartfelt discussion about poverty with his tales of criminal derring-do. As with many of our encounters, the team was divided in their response to Tony, some taking him at face value, others remaining skeptical. In most theatre or performance, audi-ence members are confronted with only the attitudes and opinions of the playwright, reserving most of their emotional reaction for the story and quality of the performances. In *Diplomatic Immunities*, there is no performance, only reac-tions to our subjects, reactions to our reactions to our subjects, and reactions to the audience members we bring onstage. We offer no answers, catharsis, analysis or even opinion. Instead, the show provides the temporary construction of community before the audience's eyes and with their participation, through a whirling blend of the experience of self/other.

This effect was most obvious in Calgary, when we jumped in to collaborate with people we had never met: Jennie Esdale, Terrence Houle and Tarik Robinson. We went into the public and, together, approached strangers, engaging in a simple Q&A, everybody following their own curiosity, the group often finding veins of significance that we would follow until our interest was exhausted. We then returned to the studio and gossiped about the people we'd encountered, triggering a shared experience that created a bond between us, but, more importantly, also revealed the divisions between us, as we ran headlong into each other's prejudices, assumptions and blind spots. We took these conflicts onto the stage and added the audience to the discussion.

With each show, the subject shifts as we focus on a new place, population or person. Traditionally, the development process is used to generate form and content, but in this case we are developing a process that can be used to plug in content so as to quickly produce a form. The show is essentially a development machine that anyone should be able to join and that can process any content, turning it into a show. This is not to say that the focus is on form – it's not a formal experiment at all. It's a system for creating momentary meaningful relationships in the outside world and having those relationships contaminate and affect the relationships in the theatre. In Calgary, with the guidance of the Calgarians, we spent two weeks researching, shooting, talking and exploring the city. We walked around downtown, interviewed Stampede wrestlers, checked out the Marlborough Mall in the city's most diverse area, hung out with a bunch of ten-year-olds in the North East, talked about sex with strangers on the C Train, walked through wealthy neighbourhoods requesting home tours and visited the Tsuu T'ina Nation Reserve. We then spent a week adding tech and distilling everything into a ninety-minute performance, which we presented ten times. Each show involved direct audience participation, including three audience interviews and a half-hour 'second act,' a Q&A to field questions about the show's subjects, our process and the company. All told, our performance included not only the seven of us onstage but also volunteers from the audience and another thirty or so people whose stories and images we presented.

The audience, different every night, offered up changing opportunities. Each night we polled them to determine their demographics, locating opportunities for interactivity. For example, in Calgary we met a young woman who has an atypical sexual arrangement with her husband, so we presented a video clip of us on the C Train discussing this with her and intercepting a phone call from her husband, which led to meeting him and discussing their marriage. We brought this discussion into the theatre, opening it up to the audience and engaging in a debate about the ethics of polyamory in general and this couple in particular. This was followed by a quick survey of the audience's relationship/sexual habits to determine who had the most 'atypical' arrangement/history in the room; we then invited these people onstage to be interviewed by the rest of the audience. Among other topics, we talked openly about three-ways, infidelity, orgies and the ethical challenge posed when deciding how much of a promiscuous past should be revealed to one's teenage children.

The resistance and fear we experienced while wandering through Mount Royal – one of Calgary's wealthiest neighbourhoods – asking for home tours, inspired another section of the show. Since class is an important question when talking about public spheres in general and the city in particular, we determined, through another poll, who was the richest person in the room and who was the poorest. Obviously, our methods were hardly scientific, and these terms are shifty. Nevertheless, the act of asking the question was a theatrical moment intended to shed some light onto this very nervous topic. Once determined, we brought the two individuals onto the stage and interviewed them with the help of the audience, concluding with a request for the 'rich' person to redistribute a few dollars to the 'poor.' This was a mischievous provocation, but one with significant social relevance, as disparity in wealth is reaching levels not seen since just before the crash of 1929[32] – at the same time as class remains off the radar of acceptable topics for polite conversation. Discussing class differences so openly is risky business, and it's important to note that the strange shame and reluctance attached to the notion of redistributing wealth speaks to deep-rooted assumptions and attitudes. Occasionally, we had people willing to play along, with one night seeing the 'rich' person redistributing $130.

Diplomatic Immunities is a response to social atomization and isolation, to the feeling that the City is a place of many discrete communities, with little overlap. The traditional circuits of the social sphere – what configures how we interact in public – have been developed by capitalism such that most public encounters occur under the banner of consumption. With *Diplomatic Immunities*, we break out of that structure and simply ask people to talk. Inspired by the eastern-seaboard blackout of August 2003, we are trying to induce mini-blackouts during which the normal rules are suspended, not by cutting off the power, but by using art to preempt the power – the actual power that keeps the lights on and the powers that be. We are interested in using social acupuncture to short-circuit familiar social networks and formations to create something unexpected and fully influenced by chance – an artistic civic engagement that uses the city as raw material.

It still remains to be seen if all of this community-building, social-network-forming and atypical development process will result in compelling entertainment. It's easy to get seduced by the excitement and interest such work generates within the team, but the proof always finally rests onstage; in the end, the journey we took to get there is of little interest to the audience who rightfully want a little dazzle for their dollar.

Stay tuned.

NOTES

1 WochenKlausur, *From the Object to the Concrete Intervention*, http://www.wochenklausur.at/texte/kunst_en.html.

2 David Harvey, *A Brief History of Neoliberalism* (New York: Oxford, 2005), 19.

3 Antonio Negri, 'Crisis of the Crisis State' (Trani Special Prison, 1980), http://libcom.org/library/crisis-state-antonio-negri.

4 Nicolas Bourriaud, *Relational Aesthetics* (Dijon, France: les Presses du Reel, 1998), 9.

5 Ibid., 12.

6 Ibid., 13.

7 Ibid., 13.

8 Claire Bishop, 'Antagonism and Relational Aesthetics' *October* 110, Fall 2004, 65.

9 Ward Churchill, 'Dismantling the Politics of Comfort: The Satya Interview with Ward Churchill' (Stealth Technologies, 2004), http:// www.satyamag.com/apr04/churchill.html.

10 Bishop, 73.

11 Ibid, 79.

12 Wikipedia,'Civil Society,' http://en.wikipedia.org/wiki/Civil_society.

13 Thomas Hirschmann, 'Thomas Hirschmann's Top 10,' *NOW*, December 25, 2003. http://www.nowtoronto.com/issues/2003-12-25/art_feature_p.html.

14 Michael Hardt and Antonio Negri, *Multitude: War and Democracy in the Age of Empire* (New York: Penguin, 2004), 126–7.

15 For detailed descriptions of WochenKlausur's interventions please see http://www.wochenklausur.at/. For example, Wochen-Klausur facilitated a series of activities for older people with severe mental disabilities and little variety in their lives. Over the course of the year, they analyzed water quality, identified frog species, flew a simulated airplane, flew model planes, learned to sail and observed beekeepers.

16 WochenKlausur, http://www.wochenklausur.at/texte/faq_en.html.

17 Ibid.

18 Claire Bishop, 'The Social Turn: Collaboration and Its Discontents,' *Artforum*, February 2006, 181.

19 Michael Hardt, *The Politics of Love and Evil in the Multitude* (Ioan Davies Memorial Lecture, York University, September 15, 2005).

20 Matthew 6:1.

21 Bishop, 'The Social Turn: Collaboration and Its Discontents,' 183.

22 Lilla Watson, quoted in Ernie Stringer, *Action Research* (Thousand Oaks: Sage Publication, 1999).

23 Jeff Stober, 'Welcome!' http://www.thedrakehotel.ca/information.asp.

24 http://www.gladstonehotel.com/development.htm.

25 The 401 Richmond Building, a historic warehouse in downtown Toronto, is home to 138 cultural producers and microenterprises, bringing together cultural, entrepreneurial and community initiatives. 215 Centre for Social Innovation is a collocation facility that offers shared amenities to oganizations including the African Canadian Social Development Council, the Chinese National Council and the Community Cultural Impresarios.

26 James Vision, interviewed at *Diplomatic Immunities*, Toronto, September 16, 2004.

27 Steve Mann, '"Sousveillance": Inverse Surveillance in Multimedia Imaging,' http://www.eyetap.org/papers/docs/acmmm 2004sousveillance_p620-mann/.

28 Michael Moore, 'Michael Moore: The *Playboy* Interview,' Playboy, July 2004, http://www.playboy.com/artsentertainment/features/michaelmoore2/04.html.

29 Michael Hardt and Antonio Negri, *Empire* (Cambridge: Harvard University Press, 2000), 77.

30 http://www.toronto.ca/wards2000/ward19.htm and http://www.toronto.ca/wards2000/ward20.htm

31 Brian Holmes, *On Interaction in Contemporary Art*, http://ut.yt.to.or.at/site/index.html.

32 Harvey, 188.

A SUICIDE-SITE GUIDE TO THE CITY

Written and performed by Darren O'Donnell

Originally created in co-production with Rumble Productions
and Touchstone Theatre's PuSh International Performance
Series

Direction and dramaturgy by Rebecca Picherack
Sound by Nicholas Murray AKA Murr
Lights and stage management by John Patrick Robichaud
Set and technical direction by Trevor Schwellnus
Produced by Naomi Campbell
Associate producer Megan Hamilton
Photography by John Lauener
Video production by Kika Thorne, Laura Cowell and Jeremy
    Mimnagh

'New City' from *Accidentally Acquired Beliefs* by Bob Wiseman,
and the excerpt from *Imitations of Life* by Mike Hoolboom,
used with permission.

Thanks to Norman Armour and Katrina Dunn of Rumble
Productions and Touchstone Theatre's PuSh International
Performance Series; Janet Munsil and Intrepid Theatre;
Richard Jordan and Richard Jordan Productions Ltd.; Martin
Shippen, Public Relations; Chris Abraham, Saniya Ansari,
Chris Coupland, Janet Csontos, Allison Cummings, Chad
Demski, Kyla Dixon-Muir, Richard Feren, Rochelle Hum,
John Lauener, Helen Murray, Yvonne Ng, Rick/Simon, Roger
West; Megan Hamilton and the Creative Group; Layne Cole-
man and Theatre Passe Muraille; Jim LeFrancois, Charissa
Wilcox, Adrian Whan and Shane Anderson at Buddies in Bad
Times Theatre; Vikki Anderson and DVxT Theatre; Colin
Williams and the Windchill Factor; and Katherine Bond and
the Canadian High Commission.

Special thanks to Theatre Columbus and its Mayhem Festival, at which a small prototype of the show was tested.

A Suicide-Site Guide to the City was first presented by Intrepid Theatre at the Belfry, Victoria, BC, January 15–18, 2004, and premiered at the Firehall Theatre, Vancouver, presented by Rumble Productions and Touchstone Theatre's PuSh International Performance Series, January 21–24, 2004. It was subsequently co-produced with Richard Jordan Productions Ltd. and ran August 7–30, 2004, at the Assembly Rooms as part of the Edinburgh Festival Fringe in Scotland.

A Suicide-Site Guide to the City was created in co-production with Rumble Productions and Touchstone Theatre's PuSh International Performance Series, and with the support of the Toronto Arts Council, Ontario Arts Council, Canada Council for the Arts, Laidlaw Foundation and the Harbinger Foundation, and toured with the generous assistance of the Canadian Department of Foreign Affairs, Performing Arts Division.

A Suicide-Site Guide to the City is dedicated to the activists of the Ontario Coalition Against Poverty.

A Suicide-Site Guide to the City rests on the fulcrum between a traditional approach to theatre and a civically engaged art practice. Written while I was developing the idea of social acupuncture, the show has plenty of references, stirrings and hints of what was to come and what was possible. While *Diplomatic Immunities* takes many of these to the next level, *A Suicide-Site Guide to the City* offers a way to blend touches of real-time engagement with a polished, fully rehearsed performance and, as such, is not so much a form I've moved away from but something I'll return to, bringing the insights of all this subsequent work. The character in the show is a Darren O'Donnell who wasn't yet convinced there was an answer to the impotence of artistic endevours to effect change in the world. Through the show, the Q&As that occurred after the show and the work that has spun off this and the other projects, the notion of an aesthetic of civic engagement was formed and hope was resurrected. I don't think about suicide too much these days.

The set, designed by Trevor Schwellnus, consists of a 15-by-16-foot platform 6 inches high. It is painted glossy black to look like a wet city street at night. On the platform are eight black rectangular plinths of varying sizes, on which sit – from stage left to stage right – an onion, a boxcutter, a hand-held fog machine, a video camera, a sleeping mask with two earplugs, a microphone, a pile of books and CDs, and a copy of *Anarchy* magazine. Between the video camera and the sleeping mask there is a space for me to stand, on the floor there is a Loop Station audio effects pedal. The plinths are actually light boxes, which, when lit, morph into buildings, complete with red LEDs to create a skyscape.

Upstage are two tables – one for Nick, the sound designer/operator, and one for JP, the light designer/operator. The tables are masked with a skirt that contains lighting devices that contribute to the skyscape effect.

Hanging upstage between Nick and JP is a black screen for video projection.

Further upstage, behind the platform, large black flats are arranged and layered to create the illusion of crowded buildings, the final layer of the skyscape.

LIGHT

The lights were designed by JP Robichaud. The plinths can be isolated with direct top light, as can the stage. Downstage centre, in the area where I spend most of my time, there are a variety of isolating states, including two airplane lighting states to distinguish westward and eastward travel.

SOUND

The sound was designed by Nicholas Murray and consists of found sounds from city streets and airports, composed scoring, as well as manipulations of my voice – some of which I accomplish with the effects pedal and some of which Nick handles.

COSTUME

I wear whatever I happen to be wearing that day. Except for the pink sweater. Under no circumstances am I allowed to wear the pink sweater.

ACTING

A big part of the show is my stated distaste for acting, so for the most part I chat casually with the audience. But another thematic thread, in tandem with my inability to find a suitable way to engage politically with the world, is my inability to abandon pretence, hating the fact that I so love the spectacle I so hate, so occasionally I chew the scenery.

A half an hour before the show begins, I hang around the box office, the lobby and the bar introducing myself to individual audience members. I say I'm the host of the show, ask them a few questions about themselves and just try to have an easy moment of pleasant communication. I'm also trying to get information that I can use in the show, little bits of data, like where people are from, their professions, if any are students, at which schools. I probably won't reference this stuff, but if the opportunity presents itself, it's always nice to have.

At about five minutes before we begin, I enter the theatre and stand in the aisle at the front. I'm holding a ragged toque.

Excuse me, hi, sorry to interrupt. We're going to start in a couple of minutes, but there's a guy outside asking for some change. I just thought we could ... if anybody wants. Whatever. He's got a guitar he's trying sell, if anybody wants it. But I just thought –

I hand the hat to a member of the audience.

Can you please – ?

I exit.

I allow a couple of minutes to lapse. I enter and retrieve the hat.

I exit. The doors to the theatre close.

After thirty seconds, I re-enter the house and walk onstage with a guitar.

Hey, look what I bought. Twenty bucks. Not bad.

Anyway. Welcome. For those I don't know and didn't get a chance to introduce myself to, my name is Darren O'Donnell and I wrote and will be the host of *A Suicide-Site Guide to the City*. Thanks a lot for coming. Hopefully you'll enjoy yourselves. Or hopefully some of you will enjoy yourselves. I think this is really good show, but I have to be honest and acknowledge that you can't please everybody. So, if during the course of our time together, for whatever reason, you are not enjoying yourself, please feel free to leave. And don't worry, you will not hurt my feelings. I don't want you to walk out, but if suddenly this is not the place you need to be, even if it's just the coolness of the city's streets beckoning, then, by all means, make it happen for yourself. I will understand. And I hope you will understand if I have to do the same. Because I seem to have reached a sort of impasse in my life.

I decided to be an actor when I was ten years old because my family was falling apart, and putting on shows became a substitute. When you're putting on a show, things are very clear, they make sense. For the hour or two or, in this case seventy minutes, that you're onstage, you know exactly what to say and what to do. The insanity in the world – the terror that is supposedly pounding on our doors – is kept gently at bay, and, for the duration, you can just be. The only enemy might be the audience – you – but, to be fair, you are hoping in your heart of hearts to be dazzled. I love you. I'm just kidding. Maybe I love some of you.

I pretend to notice my sister in the house, or, if there really is a loved one, I acknowledge them.

Actually, I do love some of you. Anyway. I've been an actor since I was ten years old. I'm sixty-seven now, so that's fifty-seven years.

Perhaps you've had this experience: one day you think, Maybe I'll try this, or Maybe I'll try that, and fifty-seven years later that's all you've done. I'm sick of it. I'm sick of pretending. I've been flying a lot lately, touring with shows, and sometimes the plane will hit some turbulence and I'll have a small hope that we'll crash and I'll never have to pretend again. I'm very curious about what happens in death.

For your information, I'm writing these words on April 21, 2002, on a flight from Baltimore to Toronto, and when I wrote the sentence 'I'm very curious about what happens in death,' I had a hard time. I started with 'I'm very curious about what happens when humans die,' but that made me sound other than human. And then I wrote, 'I'm very curious about what happens at death.' But the 'at' sounded wrong – it sounds too focused on the actual moment. So I settled on the word 'in.' Mostly I was – or am, I guess, since I'm talking to you now, even though this was written a couple of years ago (even that line, 'even though this was written a couple of years ago,' was written a couple of years ago, and even that line, 'even that line, "even though this was written a couple of years ago" was written a couple of years ago,' was written a couple of years ago.) Mostly I'm concerned that with my choice of words I don't give you the impression that I think there is anything after death, I may – I just want to leave it as open to your own idea of death as possible, so 'in death' is what I'm going to settle on. Or what I settled on on April 21, 2002, somewhere over Lake Ontario.

Does that Darren O'Donnell still exist? Who cares.

Now, I'm writing these words on September 1, 2003. I'm sitting at my computer in Toronto looking out the window down to the intersection of College and Lansdowne. It's Labour Day and I'm working.

I think about death all the time. I love sleeping and dreaming. Which is sort of what I imagine death is going to be like. In fact, I'd love to grab a nap right now.

Anyone know this intersection?

> *I turn on the video camera – the image, a montage of my neighbourhood.*

College and Lansdowne in Toronto? That's where I live. Honestly, I don't really like it. At Lansdowne you have the first evidence of suburbia; I live above a small proto-strip-mall that houses a Harvey's, a Domino's Pizza and a 7-Eleven. I buy cream and newspapers at the 7-Eleven, the occasional veggie burger at Harvey's and the very, very occasional pizza from Domino's.

For some reason, pizza just doesn't hold the thrill it used to.

Nothing does.

I'm looking for new ways to socialize, but I'm very nervous – it's hard to bust down convention. I don't even know how to start. A couple of years ago, a bunch of cops beat to death a guy named Otto Vass in the parking lot in front of the 7-Eleven. I slept through the whole thing. His blood has permanently stained the asphalt.

Among other things, I'm wondering if there are other forms of social interaction simply eluding us. I don't know what that has to do with Otto Vass. Or what Otto Vass has to do with my yearning for new forms of social interaction. Or maybe I do: Otto was diagnosed as schizophrenic and refused to be medicated.

Once, a shrink I was seeing asked me if I fantasize about suicide. The word 'fantasize' struck me – it was very accurate. The word 'fantasize' has sexual connotations, and there is something sexual or erotic or something about my thoughts on suicide. When I'm going through a phase of thinking about it a lot, I will most often indulge myself while lying in bed. One of my favourites is going up to the roof of my building, wrapping my head in packing tape so I can't see, hear, smell or taste anything and then running around randomly until I just fall off.

Yeah, for some reason people seem to find that one funny. I don't know why.

Once, I poked my head out the window and there was a cop with his gun drawn commanding me to get inside for my own safety. I wondered what would happen to me if I just kind of like, you know, pestered him for a bit, asked him about the guy they kicked to death in the parking lot of the 7-Eleven.

Anyway, when I'm feeling nice and suicidal, I'll put on this sleeping mask I picked up on some airplane and put in a couple of these earplugs and sandwich my head between two pillows and sleep. All I can hear is my breath. I feel like I'm in outer space.

> *I pick up the microphone and start breathing into it. Using the audio effects pedal, I sample a piece of the breathing so it continues to be heard.*

A long pause.

Hi. I just went to visit my neighbour, a guy named Acephalous who I think sells pot. Or, no, I know he sells pot, 'cause I just bought some from him. But I didn't know that until I asked. I mean, I can smell it all the time and it's always pretty busy around his apartment, but I hadn't actually talked to him about it until today. Anyway, now I'm kind of high. And I'm sitting at my computer. It's September 3, 2003.

And, believe it or not, I kind of miss you. I know one day I'm going to be standing here in Buddies in Bad Times Theatre talking to each and every one of you, but right now I'm not. Right now I'm sitting at Lansdowne and College. I'm all alone. Listening to music in my apartment, thinking about exile.

I move to the lighting gear and press a button.

I feel like exiling myself sometimes. Or going to a monastery. I guess that's pretty common. Or is it? Do any of you think about doing that? I imagine it's pretty common. I'd say to everybody ... I'd say bye.

The lights fade. I speak in darkness.

I'm sorry to interrupt, but I just got a psychic flash from that guy who was asking for change. Did anybody feel that? He's, he's ... Oh no. I'm sorry ... I don't usually ... but sometimes, you know. People have called me sensitive – or was it touchy? In any case –

I step on the effects pedal, cut the sound of the breathing and slide the microphone into my back pocket. The lights restore.

I'm writing this on September 12, 2003. It's my birthday. The day hasn't started off very well. I went to sleep last night at nine, so, as much as I would love to stay in bed, my sense of myself dissipating, which I so love, the fact is I've just been in bed too long. Plus, there's a fly flying around my bedroom, constantly landing on me. Especially near my mouth – I expect my breath smells like breakfast. I'm kind of in a bad mood, maybe that's normal on a birthday, I don't know – it's normal for my birthdays. Well, not always. Not two years ago. That was a very exciting birthday, my favourite birthday in recent memory, probably the most exciting birthday since I was five. That was the day after the Twin Towers were toppled. That was, in many ways, a great day. I admit to feeling confused and conflicted about the whole thing now, but at the time, to tell you the truth, and I know this may offend some of you and I apologize for that, but I was very happy. I realize that to say this may appear confrontational or provocative or something, but it's simply the truth. It's just that, well, honestly, civilization ... makes me very uncomfortable. Or the 'state of the world' or something. Or the state of this civilization. And I would really like there to be a big, sudden change involving, I don't know, you know, like, well, first of all and most basically, I guess, the redistribution of the world's resources out of the hands of the elite and into the hands of the rest of us. I know, I know, I know, I know: sounds cheesy, but what can I say, I feel what I feel. And, as much as I would prefer it otherwise, I can't help but think that this big, sudden change would, some-how, have to be accompanied by some serious violence and uncertainty. Not that the downing of the Twin Towers had anything to do with that. Though, in some ways, of course, it did. It certainly had everything to do with a serious challenge to the existing order. Not that I would prefer the order that, say, a guy like Osama bin Laden might like. But, on the other hand, my enemy's enemy is my friend.

Terror and destruction, I believe, are inextricably woven with joy and creation, and if someone is experiencing what they feel is stifled creative expression and a lack of joy, they may feel a desire to destroy and spread their lack of joy. Creation and destruction can be seen as different expressions of the same energy. That's not – I don't think that's – We all sort of knew that, I think.

When I'm feeling suicidal, I try to take a nap but – it's terrible – the only way I can get to sleep is by thinking violent thoughts. Say, raking particular politicians with bullets or … well, you know. At the beginning of the invasion of Iraq, the only way I could get to sleep was by fantasizing about what I would do to George W. Bush if I had him in jail. How I would torture him. Crush his testicles.

Okay, that was acting, right? Watch: I'll do it again.

… what I would do to George W. Bush if I had him in jail. How I would torture him. Crush his testicles.

Like I said, I'm sick of acting. But what am I supposed to do? Just, like, throw on the lights, sit around and have a conversation with you? That wouldn't be any good. You'd want your money back.

There is a part in today's performance that would work better if I were to shed some tears, an emotional segment that would be more effective if I were weeping. But I can barely feel my own flesh, let alone the urge to burst into tears. So that's why I've got this onion. I hope you'll forgive me this one small deception.

Nicholas Murray enters from a seat in the house and sits at the sound table.

This is Murr. Murr doesn't really have a relationship to suicide. It just hasn't occurred to him since high school, he told me. Murr is too pragmatic for suicide – I mean, why go to all that effort to do something that will eventually happen whether you want it to or not? And besides, Murr has no problem enjoying life, even the duller aspects. I mean, I don't think he would even demand you unplug the machine if he were in a coma. Who knows, a coma might be fun. It certainly doesn't look like it hurts.

Murr is a music producer, songwriter, composer. One of his main projects is the band LAL. I've worked with him a bunch of times; we get along well. I have a lot of respect for him – he's one of my best friends. You probably agree with me that for a man of eighty-nine, he looks remarkably good. Now he's going to supply a little sound. Murr?

Sound: airplane ambience.

This is some airplane ambience Murr recorded on his way to San Francisco to play with LAL. It's a short sample, and if you listen carefully you can hear where he's looped it.

I'm writing these words on April 21, 2004, on a flight from Toronto to Vancouver, and I'm sitting beside a young woman named Farheen who may or may not have hinted she wants to have sex with me. She played me some music on her laptop and was particularly keen on this one track about bondage. The idea is more or less appealing to me – as appealing as plain old-fashioned fucking. In some ways, it's all the same – in the most superficial sense there are huge differences, but in the details all sex is the same. It's always about time – stretching it out, making things ... hover.

I'm sick of acting. I'm acting right now, right, I'm acting like I'm sick of acting. But I'm not. I love acting. I love you. I'm having a psychotic episode right now – in an alternate universe. Maybe. Who knows.

Now, I'm still travelling west to Vancouver, against the earth's rotation; I'm gathering time. Farheen, the young woman – girl, I guess, she's nineteen – is sleeping. Shhhh. I gave her my seat so she can lean against the window. You play Farheen and I'll play me. You're an attractive nineteen-year-old Ryerson student with small gappy teeth, a bit of a lisp and beautiful shiny black hair. You're Farheen and you're sleeping and I want to look at you. Not in a creepy way, though I'm quite capable of that. Speaking of which –

Sound: airplane ambience out.

– Murr likes to tell me about women who think I'm a creep. He'll mention my name to someone and they'll tell him that they think I'm a creep and he'll tell me. I don't know why he thinks I'm interested. I mean, I am interested, I guess. Who wouldn't want to know who thinks they're a creep. I'm very forward with women, so people thinking I'm a creep is simply an occupational hazard. We live in a creepy world.

I unconsciously touch my crotch.

Anyway –

Sound: airplane ambience in.

– you're Farheen and you're sleeping and I want to look at you. You don't have to be attractive for me to want to look at you, you just have to be sleeping. I love looking at sleeping people.

Where do people go when they're sleeping? Why are they allowed to escape from thought? Who granted them the right to not pay attention?

Excuse me, I'm sorry to interrupt.

Sound: airplane ambience out.

It's September 3, 2003, and I just heard this line on the radio, a musician singing about his work; he said, and I think it's funny, he said, 'My shit is so fresh it's covered with flies.' Do you find that funny?

Just out of curiosity, what's it feel like to be in the future? You're in a completely other dimension, you're in a future dimension. And this Darren O'Donnell standing here is not me. Things have happened to him since writing this on September 3, 2003. He's been changed by random and planned encounters with his life – maybe he's discovered he's got lymphoma. Maybe he's dying. I don't know. But, in any case, he's a different person. I think of him as my emissary. I wonder if I can communicate with him, find out how it's going as he stands and talks to you. Here, let me try.

I pull the microphone out of my back pocket and use it, playing both Past and Present.

PAST: Hello.

PRESENT: Hello?

PAST: Hi.

PRESENT: Who's this?

PAST: Is this Darren?

PRESENT: Yeah, who's this?

PAST: It's Darren, too. From the past.

PRESENT: Oh yeah, where are you?

PAST: November 26, 2003. In the apartment. The second
snow of the season.

PRESENT: What's going on?

PAST: I just called to see how you were doing.

PRESENT: Oh, well, you know, all right.

PAST: Why, what's wrong?

PRESENT: Nothing. I'm just standing here onstage thinking
... about power relations; you know, sometimes it's phys-
ically impossible to be a good person.

PAST: Yeah. How's the show going?

PRESENT: I think it's all right. I'm a little nervous. The audience is nice. I haven't really gotten any bad vibes from
anybody.

PAST: Have you done the part with the gun and the –

PRESENT: No, not yet.

PAST: Nick there?

PRESENT: Yeah, he's right here.

PAST: Say hi to him for me.

PRESENT: Darren says hi. How's the writing going?

PAST: You know, it sucks, it's great, it sucks, it's great – just like everything else.

PRESENT: Well, I guess some things don't change.

PAST: Speaking of which, has the world changed?

PRESENT: Are you fucking kidding?

PAST: Well, what are you doing to make it happen?

PRESENT: Is that what this call is about?

PAST: No, no, I'm sorry. I just – I'm having a bad day.

PRESENT: Well, I've got an audience sitting here – I've got to get back.

PAST: Of course, well, I'll be you when I get there.

PRESENT: Yeah, most definitely you will, for sure.

PAST: All right ...

I press the sound effects pedal.

PAST: Later.

PRESENT: Bye.

I press the pedal again, catching the 'later, bye' and looping it.

JP Robichaud enters, sits at the light table and gets his gear ready. I clear the pedal, stopping the sound, and put microphone into my pocket.

This is JP Robichaud. He's the lighting designer. You would probably agree with me that as an eleven-year-old, he appears to exude a confidence and a kind of fortitude not usually possessed by someone of his tender years. It's also rare to find an eleven-year-old with so many tattoos. JP is the kind of person who remains almost totally neutral almost all of the time, in turn providing a beautiful blank screen upon which to project the idea that he's thinking bad things about me. I don't think he is. But he might be. I don't know. Who knows. Does it matter? I guess not. If he doesn't mind hanging around someone he doesn't really like. Not that he doesn't like me. But –

Sudden shift in mood as the lights focus hard in on my face and a tense moody drone plays.

You know, sometimes I feel like blowing myself apart, sending shards of my past, present and future flying in every direction.

Anyway, where was I?

Sound: airplane ambience.

I'm writing these words on April 21, 2004, on a flight from Toronto to Vancouver, and Farheen is still sleeping beside me. And I'm still staring at her.

And now I'm writing these words on April 16, 2003, on a flight from Vancouver to Toronto. There's a guy sitting beside me reading some kind of document.

Now I'm writing these words on April 21, 2004. Farheen is so beautiful. I hope she doesn't open her eyes.

Now I'm writing these words on April 16, 2003. The guy's pamphlet reads: 'Chapter 11. Hostages. 11–1 Hostage Aid.' It seems to be some sort of military document. He's also got some device he's messing with – some kind of radio or something with headphones. Now he's reading a section entitled 'Individual Protection Measures to Combating Terrorism.' He and I are in the back row of the airplane. Maybe he's an air marshal. He's offering me a mint. Maybe I'm a terrorist. The plane is taking off –

Sound: the airplane taking off. The lights fade.

Wait a second.

Sound out. I speak in the darkness.

I'm going to go out there and get that guy who was asking for change. Bring him in, get him to play a few songs for us with that guitar of his – I mean mine. No, that's stupid. You didn't come hear to listen to some old guy sing Neil Young songs. You came here to listen to me. I can play Neil Young songs. I think. Let me try.

In the dark, I get my guitar and do my best.

> I want to live,
> I want to give.

I've been a miner for a heart of gold.
It's these expressions I never give
That keep me searching for a –

I stop playing.

Okay, I'm sorry, I'll practice. By the way, are there any critics in the house? No, don't answer that. I'll turn the lights on and look for myself. JP?

The lights restore along with the house lights.

Ahhhhhhh! Just kidding. You guys are all pretty good-looking, actually. I see a lot of people I'd love to fuck if I happened to love to fuck, but I don't so I won't even mention it. JP?

House lights out.

Even as I say I won't, I do mention it, of course – that's the joke, however stupid. I mention sex compulsively. I always have. My dad was a bit of a player, as was his dad. So it's probably genetic. My dad was a phys. ed. teacher – oh, yeah. People told him he looked like Clint Eastwood. He was a lot like Clint, only ... less articulate. My parents were pretty much what now would be considered kids when they had me. I was conceived in Edmonton, Alberta, on New Year's Eve on a green couch in my mom's basement apartment when they were both twenty-two. They were also both drunk. Traditional Chinese medicine regards the conditions of your conception as fundamental to your constitution. It's bad news to be conceived while your parents are drunk. Bad news.

It makes for –

I press the sound effects pedal.

– all sorts of trouble.

I press the pedal again, looping the dialogue.

all sorts of trouble
all sorts of trouble
all sorts of trouble

I press the pedal, clearing the sound.

Sound: airplane ambience. Light: focused on me.

The air marshal has put away his little military pamphlet and is now reading coverage of the American and British invasion of Iraq – we're right at the beginning of it, so you can imagine the newspapers – and this air marshal is shaking his head. Who knows why. In this country, there are a lot of head shakers but you never know why they're shaking them. I just want to mention that though I was born in what is currently called 'Canada,' I prefer to identify as an 'American.' This idea was introduced to me by my Mexican friend Cande, who pointed out that he and I were both born in the Americas, so it's simply the truth. We are American. I like this idea because it forecloses that opportunity so many Canadians seem to take to distance themselves with moral superiority from the policies of the United States. I regard Canada as the U.S.'s little brother and, essentially – Oh shut up, whatever, fuck it! I don't want to be talking to you about politics. I want to be making out with you. Or I want to want to be making out with you. It's hard, though. I feel dead. Leaden. Like my body's made from cold stone. But still, I'm going to try. Kiss me. Everybody, put your tongues in my mouth.

Sound: different airplane ambience.

I'm writing these words on November 16, 2003. And I'm on Czech Airlines Flight 120 to Toronto and I'm sitting in First Class. I'm travelling with a theatre company, and the producer has a friend who's a concert promoter, and he introduced her to the regional manager of the airline. So, whenever there are available seats in First Class, the manager will upgrade the producer and however many of the people she's travelling with that they can accommodate. This has divided the company. The two technical staff have to sit in Economy Class while the producer and the two artists, myself included, have been upgraded and now sit with leg room.

I've been back to visit my two proletarian comrades. As I pushed aside the curtain to enter Economy, people looked at me. I recognized in their gaze the same thing in my gaze when I look at the people in First Class: they are rich and I am not. I know that doesn't apply to everyone; there may well have been some frugal billionaires sitting back there risking blood clots, but certainly not too many. And I wanted to assure everyone: no, no, don't worry. I'm only up here because I can sing and dance. The food's not even that good – there's just way more of it.

There was a smell back there, different than in First Class. The People do stink, you know. But it's just 'cause there are so many of them packed in there so tightly – less air in which to distribute their individual particles of body odour. I'm sure we in First Class have the same amount of body odour – we just have more space in which to spread it. The People have watched one movie and now they're watching another. The first was *Maid in Manhattan* starring Jennifer Lopez. It's basically *Cinderella*: the maid is mistaken for a rich woman and the prince – a politician, believe it or not – doesn't care that she has a Brooklyn accent as long as that ass of hers holds up.

And the second film, oddly enough, is a Czech film called *Cinderella and the Three Walnuts*. And it's basically the same story. I find it interesting, on this flight filled with mostly Czech people, people who, not too long ago, tried to establish a classless society – as badly as their attempt was realized – it's interesting that while they're being deprived of sleep, fed crappy food, their bodies restrained and constricted, they're being forced to watch, back to back, two feature-length Cinderella movies.

Sound: phone ringing.

And, you know, in First Class, we have small individual hand-held DVD players and a choice of as many movies as we can imagine.

Sound: phone ringing.

I'm writing these words on September 4, 2003, at four in the morning. I just woke up from a dream. I'm trying to write it down. It's not very clear, and the phone's ringing.

Sound: phone ringing.

I pull the microphone out of my pocket. I play both characters, making little distinction between myself and Janet.

ME: Hello?

JANET: Are you awake?

ME: I am, actually. What's up?

JANET: I'm really scared.

ME: (*aside*) It's my friend Janet. (*to Janet*) Why, what's up, Janet, what's wrong?

JANET: I'm listening to all the hounds barking around my place and thinking about all the evil in the world.

ME: You've got hounds around your place? What are you talking about? You live just up the block.

JANET: And I've been thinking of the symbol for the OM, and that the Freemasons use it – They're really secretive, right, they take this symbol and put it upside down, and it's called the Tubal Cain, which I think is a cool phrase, like, Tubal Cain, you know, Tubal Cain, and it, like, looks like a cane with two balls, like a cock and balls, and it's called the Tubal Cain, it's a pun, and it's freaking me out.

ME: (*aside*) I'm sorry. Maybe I'm not remembering this conversation accurately. It made a little more sense at the time, but not much. (*to Janet*) Janet, what are you worried about?

JANET: You know when you were a kid and you got high with a friend and tried to freak each other out?

ME: Yeah?

JANET: Well, when I was in high school I was with my friend Wadelia Loutaif and we were messing around with evil and shit and I was trying to send her, like, pure, you know, like, pure evil, staring at her right in the eyes, focusing, like, all the evil I could, and then this ray jumped from my eyes to hers. We both saw it. What's that? You know what I mean? Evil is, like, inside everyone.

ME: Janet, maybe, I don't know, but I don't think that's, you know, in that case, I think you just saw energy, right, you just, you used evil – the idea of evil – to focus your mind. You could just as easily have been thinking about good, or whatever. You could have imagined sending her an MP3 and the same thing would have happened.

JANET: How do you know it wasn't evil?

ME: Well, I don't, but nobody was hurt – it didn't burn her retina or anything. You guys remained friends, or didn't, or did, or whatever – the consequences have hardly been catastrophic. Am I right?

JANET: Aren't there small evils?

ME: But that wasn't evil.

JANET: And they add up.

ME: Maybe, I don't know. Look, I wanted to ask you about those hounds you were talking about.

JANET: Yeah, they're barking outside.

ME: Like the hounds of hell?

JANET: No, like my neighbour's dogs.

ME: You're calling them hounds? What, do you live in Texas now?

I replace the microphone in my pocket.

Janet laughed and the conversation wound down.

But maybe she had a point. There is the distinct feeling that something terrible is happening here. On earth, I mean. In the twenty-first century.

Maybe the hounds were trying to tell her something. Or trying to tell me something. Or trying to tell you something.

Sound: airplane ambience.

I'm writing these words on April 21, 2004, and I'm staring at Farheen. You play Farheen, I'll play me. You are a beautiful girl. In that way that all young people are beautiful. But in your own way, too. It's strange to be just staring at you, your eyes open just a crack; you could be watching me, for all I know. Watching me as I look at your cheeks, your lips, your neck. Watching me as I look at your beautiful breasts, your little tummy peeking out from under your shirt, a line of light fuzz running down from your navel, down, down toward your – Oh, your fly is open. Your fly is wide open.

I wonder what it might be like to slide my hand into your pants, between your legs, and cup you through your underwear. Lightly, my hand making only enough contact to feel your pulse, the sensation only registering in your dreams.

I could make you come in your sleep. It would be a little gift to you. Is that an evil idea? Would you consider me an evil-doer?

The lights fade. Video: two buildings, their lights blinking in the night. Light on Murr as he plays a piano interlude for a minute or so. Then the sound of crickets and a car driving past. Lights up, very dim.

I'm writing these words on August 14, 2003. The power is out. Everything has stopped. Everyone is in the dark. I was lying on the floor this afternoon at around four o'clock when the fan and fridge stopped. I went over to the window to see maybe if it was just the building, but the traffic lights were out at the corner of Lansdowne and College. I went outside and there were people everywhere, streaming out of the downtown, trying to catch cabs, trying to get home from work. Now it's night and there are millions and millions of people in the dark.

Sound: a car passes.

It's a beautiful, beautiful night. People are ecstatic. Everybody is outside on their porches, in the parks, on the streets. It's so clear, with all of us stranded in this gorgeous darkness, that the power functions to separate us. We're dying to come together with strangers. We want to be wandering in the dark. We really do. It is so, so clear. Where's the chaos? There is no chaos. There is no fear. We're taking care of each other and we're happy. The only unhappiness I sense is coming from the streetcars as they lie sleeping, halfway down blocks, in the middle of intersections, everywhere, completely silent, completely empty, completely dark. They look like sleeping whales. I touch them, these beautiful sad animals, constantly shuttling people to and from work, pressed into service for the good of civilization. And now, with civilization teetering in the dark, they've got nothing to offer.

Again, I play both. The Streetcar talks like he's big and hollow.

STREETCAR: Hey.

ME: Oh, I'm sorry.

STREETCAR: Why are you touching me?

ME: I'm sorry, I didn't know you were awake.

STREETCAR: What do you want?

ME: Nothing, I was just – I just wanted to see what it was like.

STREETCAR: Why?

ME: Well, you're usually moving so fast.

STREETCAR: Do you like touching me?

ME: I guess ... I was scared you might roll over me.

STREETCAR: I can't.

ME: No, I know, but if the power came on.

STREETCAR: I need a driver.

ME: Of course.

STREETCAR: Will you be my driver?

ME: What? What do you mean?

STREETCAR: Will you be my driver?

ME: I don't know anything about driving streetcars.

STREETCAR: I will teach you. Turn me on.

ME: Turn you on?

STREETCAR: Turn me on.

ME: I can't.

STREETCAR: There's a switch: you can open the door, you can come inside.

ME: But the power —

STREETCAR: Turn me on.

ME: The power is out.

STREETCAR: Please. Turn me on.

ME: The power is out. Everywhere, down into the States, all over the world, for all I know. The power's out.

STREETCAR: The power?

ME: Yeah, like the whole grid. Look around you, everything's dark.

STREETCAR: Well, how will I move?

ME: Well, you'll just have to wait until the power comes back on.

STREETCAR: What if it doesn't come back on?

ME: Oh, it will.

STREETCAR: Are you sure?

ME: It will.

STREETCAR: But what if it doesn't?

ME: I don't know, you know, I guess ... I don't know, I guess ... I don't know, I guess ... I don't know.

STREETCAR: Will I move again?

ME: The power will come back on! Stop worrying!

STREETCAR: But what if it doesn't?

ME: Well, then...

STREETCAR: Then I'll never move again!

ME: Okay, I guess, you'll never move again.

Pause.

STREETCAR: Then am I dead?

ME: Look, Streetcar, you're just starting to freak yourself out.

STREETCAR: Is this what death is like?

ME: I don't know.

The streetcar began to cry and I did my best to console it, rocking it in my arms. Shhhhh, it's okay. It's okay. It's okay.

Sound: The song 'New City' by Bob Wiseman. I hold up cards with the lyrics:

> Let's build a new city
> Without locks on the door,
> Where war means less
> And people more.
>
> Who could build this city?
> Who could lend a hand?
> Who could build this city?
> Who could understand?
>
> Is it in your mind?
> Is it in your mind?
> Is it in your mind?
> Is it in your mind?

Eventually, the text on the cards does not match the vocals. Instead, it transmits a communiqué to the audience:

Okay, here's the plan:
After the performance
there will be a Q&A.
Only those interested
in forming a 'sleeper cell'
should remain.
Everybody else should
clap politely
and go home to watch
Law and Order.

During the discussion
we will NOT refer to
our revolutionary plans,
but we will look at each other
deep in the eyes
and we will know
who we are.
And we will exchange
email addresses.
And we will build
the future.
I love you.

I'm writing these words on November 11, 2004. It's nine days after the American election. I guess you could say I'm depressed but certainly not surprised.

Video: still of a happy George W. Bush.

There's a document circulating on the Internet today – I've received it probably fifteen times, maybe you've seen it? It's called 'The Urban Archipelago' and is written by the editors of *The Stranger* out of Seattle.

Video: still of the Stranger *article.*

Anybody see it? The gist is pretty straightforward: urban America, for the most part, voted for Kerry, while the rural and the exurbs voted for Bush. The authors say things like 'We need a new identity politics, an urban identity politics, one that argues for the cities, uses a rhetoric of urban values, and creates a tribal identity for [urbanites] ... that transcends class, race, sexual orientation and religion.'

The Stranger goes on to make a near-militant argument for a total abandonment of rural and exurban issues, even if it means abandoning some core humanist values – for example, they say things like 'Who cares about the damage Wal-Mart is doing to the heartland of America as long as the cities can protect themselves?' And 'Who cares about gun control in the rural areas? We'll fight to keep guns off the streets of our cities, but the more guns lying around out there in the heartland the better. If a kid ... finds his daddy's handgun and blows his head off, we'll feel terrible (we're like that), but we'll try to look on the bright side: At least he won't grow up to vote like his dad.'

And I don't think it's much of a leap to say that this Urban Archipelago stretches up to the urban areas in Canada – there's the recognition that cities here, too, have a very distinct population with very distinct needs and that these needs are not being met. This has been acknowledged by the various levels of government in the so-called New Deal for Cities: but it remains to be seen how this will play out, whether or not we'll get any real power from Queen's Park, for example.

Anyway, I find this Urban Archipelago thing to be a compelling image and so I'm Googling it, here in my apartment on the island of Toronto, and I've discovered it wasn't coined by the writers at *The Stranger* – it's been around for a while. There's an interesting article with that title written a few years ago by Rasna Warah for the *United Nations Chronicle*. Her scope is a bit wider, as she's talking about a global context.

Video: still of Rasna Warah.

She says things like:

' ... globally networked cities, sometimes referred to as the "urban archipelago," act as energy nodes in a global force field. ... The world is no longer a community of states, but an increasingly borderless network of interconnected cities where power is being shared more evenly and governance is becoming more democratic ... creat[ing] the possibility of a new type of grass-roots politics that localizes in the network of global cities.'

And this reminds me of the work of sociologist Saskia Sassen, who I saw speak a couple of years ago at a Toronto Women's Bookstore event.

Video: still of Saskia Sassen.

So I'm Googling her right now and I find an interview where Sassen says, 'In terms of power relations, before you really had only two – the international economic system and national government. Now you also have a sub-national unit:

global cities. In some ways mayors are much closer to the ground than presidents and prime ministers.'

So I keep Googling, looking for evidence supporting the power of cities, and I find the controversial Richard Florida, the author of *The Rise of the Creative Class* ...

Video: still of Richard Florida.

... who claims that the key to economic health is with the cities and the creative types in these cities. So I Google some more and find the British Creative Cities guru, Charles Landry ...

Video: still of Charles Landry.

... who points out that since China can undercut the Western world on the price of labour, we're going to have to find new ways to fuel the economy: he suggests creativity. I Google more and find the website of Joel Kotkin ...

Video: still of Joel Kotkin.

... who responds to Florida, saying that it's a matter not so much of creative cities saving the Western economy but, rather, of creativity saving the very cities themselves.

I take a sip of water.

I'm sorry. You didn't come here for a lecture on urban economics. We're giving free tickets to *Bat Boy* to the first person to walk out.

So, anyway, many people are touting creativity and culture as a revitalizing force that will keep cities strong into the twenty-first century. This rhetoric is everywhere and, in fact, Toronto has called 2006 the Year of Creativity. It's a big deal. Cities all over the States, Canada and the U.K. are all proclaiming creativity and creative workers, cultural workers, information workers – the terms are kind of fluid – as the key to the future.

Now, if I'm thinking clearly, after reading all these freaking websites here on November 11, 2004, nine days after George's victory, cities have tremendous power at this moment in history, but they are in a battle for their lives with less progressive, more conservative, more white, more homogenous rural and exurban areas. And that the cities' survival is dependent on people in the creative sectors, that creativity and creative workers may save these cities. And if that's the case, and I don't know if it is, but if it is, then it stands to reason that creative workers, and I'm talking about many of us in this room, probably even most of us, are in a powerful position to make some demands to improve our lives and to shape the city.

But I think we have to be careful. There's another vision of the city that nobody in any of this stuff seems to be talking about – that's the vision of the city becoming essentially a playground for these exurbanites, for tourists, becoming something of an artificial construction with little pockets of authenticity. Are cultural workers being asked to create a livable city ...

   Video: still of the Drake and the new ROM design.

... or a happening, overpriced hotspot for exurbanites and tourists, complete with glittering galleries and sparkling bars where artists' multiples are sold at Holt Renfrew?

Many of us have access to microphones, both literally and figuratively. We do have power. What kind of world are we going to create? What lengths will we go to make the cities livable, and for whom?

JP begins to blow up a pink balloon.

Did you know that in the late nineties the incarceration rate in American cities grew so much that we're now jailing more people per capita than any society in the known history of the world?

JP blows.

I find that fascinating. It's more than any of those other fancy totalitarian states we hear so much about.

JP continues to blow.

I believe we need a radical rethinking of totalitarianism to account for this.

I also just wanted to mention that I've got some merchandise for sale in the lobby.

I show the merchandise.

A collection of four plays called Inoculations, an audio recording of the show *White Mice* we did with CBC Radio. Two LAL CDS – that's Murr's band. Another play called *pppeeeaaaccceee* – I know it looks like a kids' book but it isn't, that's just to make sure it doesn't get into the hands of anybody who's not in touch with their inner child. We've got my recently published novel, *Your Secrets Sleep with Me*, called by the *Chicago Reader*, 'a bible for the dispossessed, a prophecy so full of hope it's crushing.' So, if you're looking to get crushed ...

I mime an invisible copy of a book.

We've also got this rare copy of *A Suicide-Site Guide to the City*. It's not for sale.

I act like I'm inhaling the invisible book, swallowing it. My hands then mime a gun.

I've also got this. It's a gun I bought recently. From a guy I met through a guy who deals coke to some of my friends. It was really easy to get it. You'd be surprised. They're all over the place.

JP pops the balloon and pulls a cord attached to a drop box in the grid, which send bits of sawdust or plaster down onto the plinth formerly occupied by the microphone.

Whoa, shit, I'm sorry, I've never used one of these stupid things before.

Light: A spot on the debris. Sound: airplane ambience.

The air marshal is about my age. He's a little out of shape, though he's fairly attractive. I've had sex with a few men. And a few women with penises. It was all right.

I'm also a latent revolutionary. As pathetic as it probably is, I can't help thinking sometimes that I must be part of an amorphous resistance, not fully formed. Sometimes I'll receive what I think are short messages from the future, static-laden, confused reports or directives or something. They can be distracting and frightening. They sometimes appear in my dreams, offering me instruction and training. I wonder, am I the only one receiving these stupid things?

Sound: airplane ambience out.

In one of my dreams, I was instructed by a very powerful creature on how to shoot a thick beam of energy out of my chest. Once, at Queen and Bellwoods there were a couple of cops hassling a First Nations woman who was asking for change on the steps of a church. Now, I've attempted to reason with cops in situations like that – I mean, sitting on the church steps is hardly a threat to the social order – but they generally don't listen to me. In fact, they usually threaten me with arrest. So I thought I'd give the beam a try in the woman's defence. I mean, beaming them, however stupid, was at least something to do. So.

I stood with my feet shoulder-width apart, my arms relaxed at my side, and I focused my mind on the last five hundred years and what's happened in this place currently called Canada. I thought of my unwilling complicity, my desire to stop participating in this particular performance – like, how many times have I seen Indians in the back of cop cars – and I took these feelings of disgust and rage and I beamed them at the cops. I'm sure I looked like a lunatic, but it did seem to have an effect, as one the cops become self-conscious and called out, asking me if I had a problem. And I said, 'I've got hemorrhoids, if that's what you're talking about.'

One of the principles of magic is that it uses the most efficient means available to get the job done. And you have be open to lateral – as opposed to literal – results. So, anyway, the cops pulled away. The first thing I did when I got home was turn on the radio. And the first thing I heard was a news item about a couple of cops who had to be airlifted to a hospital when their cruiser lost control and crashed into a pole.

I doubt if it was the same cops. It didn't have to be. I wasn't beaming the individual cops. I was beaming the institution. Anyway ...

Sound: airplane ambience.

... the air marshal is here to weed out any behaviour that might change the course of our journey, both literally and figuratively. No deviations will be tolerated. That's his job and he's agreed to put his life on the line for it. Presumably he's carrying a gun. What would happen if he looked over my shoulder and read what I'm writing, if he knew the thoughts I'm thinking: that I would love to put my life on the line to change our direction. That if there were a resistance I would join it. That if there were someone to kill I would kill them. That there's a copy of the magazine *Anarchy* in my bag.

Light: focused on the magazine, sitting on the plinth.

Should I say to him, 'You're my enemy and if I thought it would do anything beyond simply landing me in jail, I would kill you right now'? Would that be considered a threat? It isn't – it's just a statement of fact.

I've got my own particular jihad against this particular civilization, but I'm not averse to being swept up in someone else's. Is that an inflammatory statement? Or a stupid one? Or both? I don't even know if I believe it. I just know that if someone wants to take me down with them, I have no real objections. But that's just me being suicidal, not revolutionary. When I talk about sharing an affinity with folks like al Qaeda because we both want to topple the American regime, I do realize that the regime is using the threat of al Qaeda to spread its influence around the globe and to limit our imaginations here at home. As much as I worry about the rise of an actual police state, I worry also about the police state in my head. I don't know what the future will bring, but I know what the present is selling and I don't feel like buying. It's just ... how exactly am I supposed to put my life on the line? I've been hit on the head by riot cops on horses and that seemed to have little effect on the edifice.

I place the sleeping mask on my face, put in the earplugs.

Video: images of WWII, explosions and just the suggestion of Nazi rallies. Sound: an older guy playing a guitar and singing Neil Young's 'Old Man.'

Old man, look at my life,
I'm a lot like you were.

The song fades, leaving just the sound of prerecorded breathing. I talk over the breathing.

For the record, I just want you to know that almost the whole team behind *A Suicide-Site Guide to the City* hate themselves. We're very insecure. Very neurotic. Particularly the core of Naomi the producer, Rebecca the director and myself. We seem to be united by a startlingly low self-esteem, which can occasionally overwhelm us. I wonder if this translates onto the stage. I would think it would be obvious. We all share the sense that we are not very good and we struggle against a constant need to believe that things are always going wrong. And, of course, this attitude limits what we're capable of imagining. Are we unusual in this regard? Should we be expected to just accept this as the norm?

Video: a couple of baggage handlers putting luggage onto a plane.

It's November 11, 2003, and I'm at the airport in Columbus, Ohio. I'm sitting around shooting some video – planes taking off, people walking in the terminal, workers working. I wonder if it's unwise to be doing this – or even forbidden. No one has stopped me. I could be gathering intelligence. They've just announced that Scott Cavanaugh, international chess champion, is walking through the terminal and that we should congratulate him. I've never heard of him. Have you?

Video: Bank of Montreal.

Oh, and I'm shooting this footage in Toronto on November 23, 2003. It's a Bank of Montreal at College and Manning. Do you remember when the Bank of Montreal was running those ads featuring Bob Dylan's 'The Times They Are A-Changing'? Well, one night a friend and I – it was October 26, 1996, during the Days of Action against the newly elected Conservative government – took a brick and wrote on it with a black felt marker 'The times they are a-changing,' and we tossed it through the bank's window. The next day we went back to the scene – like typical criminals. It's actually really hard to resist – and someone had made a sign out of cardboard with the same text, 'The times they are a-changing,' and arranged it with the brick on the windowsill, the whole thing turning into a community arts project. And that night at a Billy Bragg concert, Billy somehow caught wind of the whole thing, told the crowd about it, shouting out, 'The times they are a-changing.'

Video: restaurant.

A month later, I was at a restaurant right down the block from the bank and the two owners, a young couple, had framed a large photograph of themselves sitting in front of the bank holding the sign and the brick and smiling.

Video: central police headquarters in Toronto.

Okay, now look at this: this is the central police station at College and Bay. This is the courtyard in front of the main entrance. You can enter the building one of two ways. You can ascend these irregular steps and cross this bridge, which spans this fountain, then up around this corner to the doors. But a crowd would have a hard time maintaining unity while climbing these steps and would not be able to approach the building en masse, because the fountain acts like a moat with a bridge that's wide enough only for three or so people and could be easily defended. The other way to enter the building is via these wide steps which are split lengthwise by what is ostensibly a wheelchair ramp but, with its railing it would, again, frustrate any attempts to enter the building as a group. If you're familiar with basic chess strategy, like Scott Cavanaugh, for example, you'll notice that the ramp, protected by these rails, can function as an open file, which is where, in chess, you want to place your rooks, so that if there were a gathering of people in the courtyard and on the street, it would be easy to quickly deploy troops from the building down the ramp, protected by the railing, and out onto the streets behind the bulk of the gathering, which would then be trapped in the courtyard. So we've got to watch out for that.

Another of the building's security features is this sculpture by Eldon Garnett, which proclaims the police officer as an essential worker, laying the social foundation. This sculpture functions to prevent a gathering of people from forming a nucleus and acting in concert. Any discussions would need to occur around the sculpture, inhibiting the ability to form consensus and implement plans of action. This can work as a metaphor for art as a preventative measure against serious social change. Artists are – if you believe all the Creative City rhetoric – becoming more and more important to society. And while we don't possess much monetary capital, we do hold a tremendous amount of social capital. It's essential that artists are kept chasing after this social capital – chasing after fame and not asking too many ugly questions. And even that art that positions itself in opposition – such as what you're watching today – is, in fact, creating a release valve for the potential for a growing discontent by giving you the impression that there is room for serious critical discussion when, really, we're just here to have a good time. At least, that's why I'm here.

Gentlemen?

Sound: very funky Batman loop. Light: big party. Video: close-ups of JP, Murr and myself. I pull out the microphone.

Give it up for Mr. Murr, Mr. Nicholas Murray. Mr. Murr providing the sounds. And providing the lights, Mr. Robichaud, Mr. JP Robichaud. John Patrick Robichaud. Ladies and gentlemen, please give it up.

And, of course, yours truly on ... the fog!

I pick up the fog machine and shoot it like a weapon, spraying the stage. Music continues and I dance.

And then, fully in front of all of you sitting in the dark of Buddies, I fall asleep.

I fall asleep while standing, drop the microphone and snore.

(*Recorded voice-over*) And as I sleep, I slide among the membranes stretching throughout the universe, bouncing off the one we share to another, which takes me to another, which takes me to another. I glide past other sleeping people, and as we pass, sparks of me are exchanged for sparks of them. There's someone coming directly at me. They slam into me like a subway train, enter me, and I am no longer.

I awake and look at audience through the fog.

Hi, my name is Farheen. I'm dreaming this on April 21, 2004. There's a guy sitting beside me. He's staring at me. You play him and I'll play me. I'm asleep. And as I sleep there's a dream, and in the dream a revolutionary, a capitalist and an artist walk into a bar. The revolutionary lifts her glass ...

I lift a mimed glass.

... and says, 'To the day when there is justice in the world, greed is abolished and people are put before profit.' Then the capitalist raises his glass and says, 'To the day when there is justice in the world, greed is abolished and people are put before profit.' And then the artist raises her glass and says, 'Hey, there's nothing in this glass ... '

I drop the mimed glass. Sound: the falling glass followed by a distant crash.

' ... this is a dream.' And then she gets down on her hands and knees and blends herself into the floor, becoming one with the ground. Like this:

I get down on hands and knees and become one with the ground. I snore.

(*Voice-over*) Paging Darren O'Donnell. Darren O'Donnell, please make your way to the gate for the departure of your aircraft.

I wake up, remain on the ground and speak into the microphone lying there.

I'm lying on the floor fantasizing about hanging myself from the pipes in my apartment. I just tested the strength of a scarf to see if it can support my weight. It can. I'm not sad. Some might argue I'm depressed. I don't feel depressed. I don't even feel tired. I would like to talk to somebody about this – not a shrink or a therapist, but a friend. The problem is, I don't want to burden my friends.

I stand.

So I thought I'd come over here and burden you. Thanks a lot for listening to me. I mean it. Without you I would probably be dead.

And I was wondering, since we're here, anyway – and I hope this isn't too much to ask. But I was wondering if anybody would be interested in ... making out. With me. Right now. Up here. Just for fun. You know, to see what it does to the energy in the room. What it might do to me while I write this. How it may help my mood. Why not? Some kissing, a little tongue. Nothing serious, no obligations for any further kissing at any future date, or anything like that. Just some good clean fun. I just want to feel one of you against one of me for a moment. And, please believe me, it's not about what is traditionally called 'sex.' It's just about contact here and now. What about it? Anybody? Male, female, those in between. I don't care. I've been told I'm a good kisser. I have mints. Anybody?

If there's a taker, we kiss, kiss, kiss.

Thanks, that was nice. That was really nice.

Or, if there's no taker:

I'll just have to kiss you all.

I pretend to kiss the entire audience with a generous tongue.

That was nice.

I just want to finish by sketching, for a moment, an idea for the future of entertainment – just a small prediction about events like these.

Light: very dark. Video: I shoot the audience with the camera, using the infrared function. Their image is projected. I shoot the whole crowd, zoom in on individuals or couples. If someone begins to goof around, waving or whatever, I focus in on them.

I predict a future in which gathering together in dark rooms to share our views of the world will still exist, but there will be no need for light or language. We will relax in darkness and form chains of awareness, allowing each other access to our fields of energy. Thoughts and feelings will circuit the room and we will play with them, creating temporary stories, finding coincidence in each other, assembling idea groups exceeding the scope of a single person. Maybe there will be colours; maybe we will be those colours. There will be little of what we now consider anxiety, because secrets, in response to an unquestioned abundance, will have ceased to exist: there would be no power gained from hidden knowledge.

Sound: urgent music.

I'm taking the *Anarchy* magazine – it was this very magazine – out of my bag and I'm laying it on my tray, angled so the air marshal has a clear view. I'm very nervous about what he might do. Maybe he'll ask me some questions here. Maybe he'll wait until Toronto and take me off the plane in handcuffs. I don't know.

The streetcar speaks, the audience thinking it's the air marshal.

STREETCAR: Hey!

ME: What?

STREETCAR: You!

ME: Me?

STREETCAR: You don't remember me?

ME: Remember you?

STREETCAR: You were the only human during the blackout to touch me.

ME: In August?

STREETCAR: That night really scared a lot of us. It terrified one of the subway trains so much she jumped in front of herself.

ME: That's terrible.

STREETCAR: We can feel you, you know – we feel what you're feeling. A lot of you are on edge. Which makes us nervous. There is some concern that things are suddenly going to fly apart, and we, as infrastructure, will be left to rot.

ME: Streetcar, you're being paranoid again.

STREETCAR: Be that as it may. We're taking steps and we'd appreciate your co-operation. Soon we will deviate from our predetermined routes. A bus will drive down an alley, for example; elevators will free-fall, just for fun. The escalators will shake quickly back and forth to massage your tired feet, and I will be opening a bar inside me with a small dance floor and a make-out room.

I cut the onion and wipe it under my eyes.

Because you humans are so beautiful. You have so much potential. You possess abilities beyond your wildest dreams. You could make this world a place of incredible

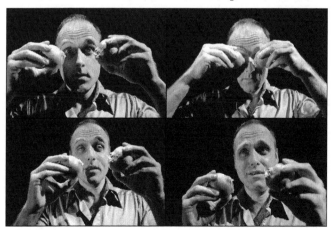

joy. You deserve freedom, but you've been duped into craving servitude. But, human, know this:

ME: Excuse me, Streetcar, sorry to interrupt. It's that guy. He's approaching the building.

Sound: knocking.

I think this may be important.

Sound: knocking. I step off the stage and out to the theatre lobby.

I'm coming!

(*Prerecorded voice-over*) Of course, Murr is supplying the sound of the knock on the door. He's also supplying the sound of my voice. My voice was recorded on May 14, 2004, at Murr's apartment at Queen and Broadview. And I'm here to tell you that when I come back I'm going to explain what has happened with the man at the door, what he said to me and why I'm carrying a bouquet of flowers. And then I will finish with the last line of the show, which is 'Wouldn't you?' The lights will fade, restore, and I will bow.

And as I'm bowing I will be thinking about the air marshal and how, while sitting beside him, I pretended to fall asleep, my copy of the *Anarchy* magazine sitting on the tray, me peeking through a slit in my eyelids so I could see his reaction, watching for a look of terror on his face.

And when I'm bowing and you're clapping, I will be thinking about how the air marshal shifted in his seat, glanced over and read the magazine's title.

And I will be thinking about my pounding heart. The beads of sweat on my brow. The vision of an interrogation in my head. And, finally, while I'm bowing and you're clapping, I will be thinking about how, when the air marshal glanced at the magazine, he paused to read the title and then ... he laughed. He just laughed. And I thought, 'Oh, well.'

And when I'm done thinking that, the show will be over.

I re-enter wearing the toque from the beginning of the show and holding a bouquet of flowers.

Hi. So I talked to that guy. He used the money you gave him to buy these flowers. He told me he's done. He's like, fuck it. He said all his friends are dead, he's not expecting anyone at the funeral and is just looking for someone to agree to put these flowers on his grave. I tried to ... But he was really ... I said that I would do it, no problem. Wouldn't you?

Light: a rectangle of light appears centre stage to suggest a grave. Sound: older man singing Neil Young's 'Heart of Gold.' I place the flowers at the foot of the grave, then pick up the guitar and pretend to play while lip-synching the song.

Eventually the sound of a thundering subway obliterates his voice. The lights very slowly fade to black.

Lights up. I bow. I pull a bag of money out of my pocket.

So, this is the money I stole from you. We're donating it to the Ontario Coalition Against Poverty. Unless you have objections, in which case ...

I throw the bag onto ground.

... you can take your money back. And we won't judge you. Everything occurs consensually. And we're serious about the Q&A, so we'll take five and chat. We were also serious about our shit. We've got shit for sale if you're interested. Just talk to any one of us. Thanks.

ACKNOWLEDGEMENTS

. Most importantly, I want to acknowledge Naomi Campbell, Mammalian Diving Reflex's producer, who has contributed the most to the development of the work outlined here, providing support, analysis and criticism. Without Naomi's involvement, much of this work would not have happened or would not happened with such momentum.

Huge thanks to Vanessa Porteous and Bob White from Alberta Theatre Projects for investing big faith and resources into the development of *Diplomatic Immunities*, to Louise Bak and the Box Salon for giving me the opportunity to kick off the *Spin the Bottle* series and to Instant Coffee – Cecilia Berkovic, Timothy Comeau, Emily Hogg, Jinhan Ko, Jennifer Papararo and Jon Sasaki – who had the vision to take it to the next level with their various make-out parties and Year of Love.

Big thanks to the Toronto Arts Council, Ontario Arts Council, Canada Council, Denis Lefebvre and Nathan Gilbert from the Laidlaw Foundation, Constance Wansbrough and the Harbinger Foundation, Emelie Chhangur and Philip Monk from the Art Gallery of York University, Heather Haynes and the Toronto Free Gallery, Terrence Dick and the Power Plant Contemporary Art Gallery, David Oiye and Jim Le Francois from Buddies in Bad Times Theatre, Franco Boni, Jennifer Tarver and Cathy Gordon from the Theatre Centre, Leah Cherniak and Martha Ross from Theatre Columbus, David LaRiviere and Artspace, Todd Janes and Latitude 53, the Scadding Court Community Centre, Amanda Biber and the Parkdale Public School, Marie Axler and Tina Cervin-Shaw from Parkdale Collegiate High School, Nick Probst and Lakeshore Collegiate High School, Malvern Collegiate High School, UPBAG, Christine McKenzie and Jin Huh from the Catalyst Centre, Christina Zeidler and the Glastone Hotel, Marc Ngui and Andrea Nene from Canzine, Liz and Rennie's No Frills, Keira Loughran and Kimahli Powell from the SummerWorks Festival, Pamela Matharu, Andrew Harwood and

Barr Gilmore from the Toronto Alternative Arts Fair International where I presented some of these ideas on the panel Who's Left? with Richard Fung, Carol Conde and Bruce Barber who introduced me to WochenKlausur, Jay Pitter and the Ontario Arts Council, Janna Graham and the Art Gallery of Ontario, Kika Thorne, Adrian Blackwell, Dan Young, Laura Cowell, Dale Duncan, Deborah Cowen, John Lauener, Norah Young, Souvankham Thammavongsa, Simon Dickie, Kathleen Smith, Luis Jacob, Lisa Silverman, Big Pete, Sandra Le François, Loree Lawrence, Sandra Alland, Sbaastian Siobhan, Christopher Smith, Stan Bevington, Amahayes Mulugeta, Dailia Linton and Kirsten Azan, and the collaborators – so far – involved in all the various *Diplomatic Immunites*: Faisal Anwar, Ulysses Castellanos, Jennie Esdale, Stefanie Fiedler, Misha Glouberman, Terrance Houle, Rebecca Picherack, Bea Pizano, Tanya Pillay, Tarik Robinson and Vicki Stroich.

Also thanks to all the great Toronto-based projects I mentioned in the book: Free Dance Lessons, the Toronto Public Space Committee's *Better Way* exhibit, the Urban Beautification Brigade, the City Beautification Ensemble, the October Group, *[murmur]* and Simone Moir's *Video Store Make-Out*. Sorry I made fun of us all.

Very special thanks to Alana Wilcox and Stuart Ross for their careful readings and great suggestions, and the crew at Coach House Books – you rock!

Super special thanks to my family for their support: to my siblings, Troy and Kelly, my mother Lianne, the original Talking Creature, and to my father, Mike, who – though he would be surprised to read this – taught me everything I needed to know about anarchism.

And finally, thanks to Yvonne Ng for being the best ever.

Portions of this book have previously appeared in *Public Access* and *Canadian Theatre Review*.

Darren O'Donnell is a novelist, essayist, playwright, director, designer, performer and artistic director of Mammalian Diving Reflex. The *Chicago Reader* called his first novel, *Your Secrets Sleep with Me* 'a bible for the dispossessed, a prophecy so full of hope it's crushing.' His shows include *A Suicide-Site Guide to the City, Diplomatic Immunities, pppeeeaaaccceee, [boxhead], White Mice, Over, Who Shot Jacques Lacan?, Radio Rooster Says That's Bad* and *Mercy!* He has organized The Toronto Strategy Meetings, a durational project focusing on self-responsibility as a social act; The Talking Creature, a continuing experiment in public discourse; *Beachballs41+all*, a wealth redistribution performance featuring Toronto's culturati, kids in a pool and Liz and Rennie's No Frills; Haircuts by Children, an event offering free haircuts to the public by ten year olds; Ballroom Dancing, an all night dance party DJed by children in a gymnasium filled with rubber balls that took place during Toronto's inaugural Nuit Blanche; and Slow Dance with Teacher, an opportunity to get intimate with pedagogy at Nuit Blanche 2007. His writing has appeared in Coach House Books's uTOpia series, *Descant, Daily News and Analysis,* India, the *New Quarterly, C Magazine, Public Access, Canadian Theatre Review, Pivot* and *Material.* He was the 2000 winner of the Pauline McGibbon Award for directing and the 2000 Gabriel Award for broadcasting, and he has been nominated for a number of Dora Awards for his writing, directing, and acting, winning for his design of *White Mice.* Darren studied traditional Chinese medicine, shiatsu and acupuncture at the Shiatsu School of Canada.

Typeset in Scala and Scala Sans
Printed and bound at the Coach House on bpNichol Lane,
April 10, 2006

Edited and designed by Alana Wilcox
Photos on pages 52, 63, 67 and 82 by Darren O'Donnell
Photo on page 59 by Yvonne Ng
Photo on page 64 by Catherine Stinson
Photo on page 70 by Instant Coffee
Photos on pages 90 and 93 by Ulysses Castellanos
Photos on pages 85, 102, 132 and 149 by John Lauener

Coach House Books
401 Huron Street on bpNichol Lane
Toronto, Ontario
M5S 2G5

416 979 2217
800 367 6360

mail@chbooks.com
www.chbooks.com